TEACH YOURSELF BOOKS

ECONOMICS

Economics is the study of man in his efforts to make a living. It examines the various branches of the economic system and tries to show how they work and fit together to form a harmonious whole. This general outline aims to explain the practical importance of the subject and to clarify many problems with which the reader, as an individual and as a citizen, is faced. The Test Exercises and the Bibliography at the end of the book will be of value to those wishing to make a deeper study of the subject.

This is an ideal introduction to the principles of Economics because it simplifies what, to the man in the street, is a difficult and dull subject.

Higher Education Journal

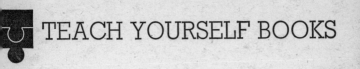

TEACH YOURSELF BOOKS

ECONOMICS

S. Evelyn Thomas
B.Com., Ph.D.(Lond.), F.C.I.S., A.I.B.

Revised by
M. Sclare
B.A. (Hons. Economics and Political Science)

ST. PAUL'S HOUSE WARWICK LANE
LONDON EC4P 4AH

First printed 1939
Revised edition 1970
Second impression (with corrections) 1972
Third impression 1973
Fourth impression 1974

ISBN 0 340 05566 9

Printed in Great Britain
for The English Universities Press Ltd.,
by Richard Clay (The Chaucer Press), Ltd., Bungay, Suffolk

INTRODUCTION

ECONOMIC problems are amongst the most pressing problems that modern communities have to deal with. Wage increase demands, constantly rising prices and costs of living, and balance of payments deficits present unceasing and urgent problems to Governments, and the advice of the economist is of great importance in helping to settle them.

A small book must of necessity be full of omissions, but it is hoped that this brief general outline of the subject-matter of Economics will help to explain the practical importance of the subject, and stimulate an interest in it that will lead to its true and proper appreciation.

This object will have been achieved if readers find from a study of this little book that Economics can help them to a clearer understanding of many problems with which they are faced, both as individuals and as citizens. And in the hope that some of them, at least, will become sufficiently interested in the subject to continue their investigations, a bibliography of larger works to which they can usefully refer is given.

CONTENTS

CHAPTER I

WHAT IS ECONOMICS?

IF we could take an instantaneous photograph of the activities of men and women at, say, 11 a.m. on any business day, we should see that the majority were engaged in one or other of a great variety of different occupations. We should see people working in shops, factories, fields and offices; on the railways and the roads; on ships at sea and in mines far below ground. We should see teachers in their classrooms, doctors in their surgeries, business men in their offices, shop-keepers attending to the needs of their customers, and civil servants busily engaged on various forms of government work.

A little reflection would show us that the activities of all these different people have two aspects in common. We should realise, first, that all these busy people are engaged in *earning their living*, and that their earnings—the reward they receive for their labours—enable them to satisfy their essential needs for food, clothing and shelter, possibly also to obtain, in addition, some comforts and luxuries, and to put something aside for a rainy day. We should realise also that these people, in the process of earning their living, are at the same time contributing to the production of goods or services needed by other members of the community.

THE ECONOMIC SYSTEM

This process of earning one's living by producing goods and services for the community is known as *economic activity*. And the whole sum of economic activities—the complex structure or mechanism whose many parts work together—form what is known as the *economic system*.

The economic system is so bound up with our lives that we are apt to take it very much for granted. But when the system is dislocated for any reason, when a strike leaves us without fuel, or a war makes it difficult for us to get food, we become painfully conscious of the economic aspect of life. We are then compelled to think of the amazingly intricate system in which we work and by which we live. Then we begin to wonder why things are not going right and why we have to suffer because of conditions with which we have little or no apparent connection. It is here that a knowledge of Economics helps us to understand the situation and to see ourselves as part of a most complex economic organisation.

Although the economic system is thus of paramount importance in our everyday life, very few of us ever bother to learn something about it. Yet it is just as important that we should understand something about Economics, which sheds light on our material life, as it is for us to understand the main principles of health and even of religion. If as thinking men and women we are to understand our position in the great scheme of things, we should know why we have to earn a living, why we enter a particular occupation, how we regulate the spending of our earnings, the organisation involved in buying the goods we need, the way in which goods produced abroad and at home are made available for us as consumers, the principles that determine the prices we have to pay for those goods and the banking and financial institutions that make it possible for the goods bought at home and abroad to be paid for. All such matters are part of the subject-matter of Economics.

The Problem of Choice

Briefly, then, *Economics is the study of man in his efforts to make a living*. It studies the various branches of the economic system and tries to show how they work and fit together to make a complete pattern. The science of Economics is based upon the facts of the ordinary, business, work-a-day world. It is the task of the Economist to describe these facts in their proper order and true perspective, so as to explain the working of the system in which we live and work.

There would be no *economic problems* and, therefore, no need for economic investigation, if our resources were large enough to satisfy all our wants; if we could get all the food, clothes and shelter we need without first having to earn the means to pay for these things. Not many of us, however, are fortunate enough to get such things for nothing; most of us have to work to obtain the "means" to buy them; we have to work to "earn our living".

Even the living we earn enables few of us to acquire *all* the things we would like to acquire. You might want an aeroplane; I might want a grand piano. But most of us have only *limited means*. In return for our labour we have only a certain amount of money placed at our disposal. Naturally, therefore, we try to spend our earnings so as to get the greatest *satisfaction* out of them. We allocate them to buying food and clothes; to paying our rent, rates and insurance; to meeting our travelling and holiday expenses. We have many things to do with our wages and they are rarely large enough to buy all the things we need. You might have to do without a holiday so that you can buy a winter coat; I might have to go without certain luxuries so that I can buy a house. Some people cut down beer expenses in order to go to the cinema; others stint themselves on clothes so as to be able to run a car.

Thus we and all our fellows are continually weighing up our want for one thing against our want for another, considering one form of expenditure against another, wondering whether to spend the odd pound note on a new hat or a new picture, on a new rug or a new bedspread.

Our time, too, is limited. We have not time to do *all* the things we want to do. We have, therefore, to allot so much of our time to working, so much to eating, so much to sleeping, so much to leisure; and, of course, the time we devote to one purpose is not available for another purpose.

The Economist sums up this position in the statement that *man is constantly confronted with the problem of choice.* Whether at home or at business, he is constantly "economising" in one direction or another. If there were no need for choosing, if we all had as much time and as ample resources as we wanted, there would be no need for "economising" and no economic problems would arise. But as things are, because *our time and our means are limited* and because there are alternative ways in which we can use them, we are continually being faced with economic problems. We are continually considering how to allocate or "economise" our resources and our time so as to get the most satisfaction from them. And such problems have to be faced as much by a Robinson Crusoe, cast away on a desert island with but a few implements and little food, as by the managing director of a great modern business, or the controller of a great railway.

Doctor or lawyer, business man or manufacturer, clerk or consumer—each is confronted with the need for making a choice. Young doctors have to decide whether to go into general practice or to spend more money on their training and so become "specialists" in a particular branch of their profession. Manufacturers have to choose between different types of possible products and have to apportion their money on machinery, raw material and labour so as to reap the greatest benefit from their expenditure. Consumers, too, have to decide how to lay out their money to the best advantage: whether to buy fish or meat, bread or potatoes, new clothes or new curtains, and in what quantities to buy any such goods as they need from time to time.

Such decisions by producer and consumer are being made so frequently that they are largely automatic and subconscious. Yet the nature and the extent of economic activity are determined by these decisions. *The choice between alternatives* is the very foundation of the economic system.

THE SYSTEM OF PRIVATE ENTERPRISE

Our economic structure is based on the system of *private enterprise*. This implies two main conditions: first, that all property can be privately owned; and, secondly, that people are *economically free, i.e.*, subject to obedience to the law, they are free to use their time and means as they like.

In this country, people own private property in numerous forms and varying amounts: some people own a house; other people own a house and a car; some fortunate few have houses, cars and yachts; others own factories, machines, mills and farms. In respect of all such properties owned by individuals, the ownership is under the protection of the State, *i.e.*, *the State protects the right of the individual* to control his property and his goods, whilst the owner whose property is stolen or damaged can call on the law to assist him to obtain redress and in some cases to punish the offenders.

Economic Freedom means that the individual is free to do as he likes with his own property and with his own time and energy. But we can see at once that, in any civilised community, there must be some limit to the exercise of this freedom. Although the individual is economically free, he must conform to the laws and regulations made by Society for the general good, otherwise we should have many abuses and great social difficulty. An owner of land, if free to do as he liked, might build a slaughter-house in Regent Street, London, or a tannery opposite the Houses of Parliament. A manufacturer, if uncontrolled by law, might make his employees work eighteen hours a day in a dangerous atmosphere with unprotected machinery, or a grocer might sell unwholesome or even poisonous food.

To avoid the possibility of such abuses, Society imposes certain restrictions. Generally, the individual is free to earn his living as he likes, to buy and sell as he likes, to use his factory and machines to produce what he likes, and to compete with his fellows. But in all such activities his freedom is subject to restrictions imposed by the State for the general good. If a man wishes to build a house or a shop, he must submit his plans to the local authority; if he wishes to sell milk or meat, he must conform with certain State regulations; if he wishes to be a doctor or a lawyer, he must submit to a certain training and comply with the rules that govern those professions.

This system of economic freedom and private enterprise does not preclude the possibility of *State* or *municipal enterprise*. In all States there is public enterprise to varying extents. It is by means of State enterprise that costly essentials of busy communities can be provided. Bridges and motorways would not be built, and services, such as education and health services, would not be forthcoming under private enterprise because the large outlay involved would not show a profit. In Britain, public enterprise covers several basic industries —coal, rail, and some other forms of inland transport, air services, gas and electricity—in addition to the Bank of England, the British Broadcasting Corporation (B.B.C.), and several local government undertakings such as baths, bus services and swimming pools.

The British economic system is a *capitalist system*, but in it economic freedom is not absolute; the system that prevails is one of *comparative* freedom. The freedom of the individual, whether acting alone or in conjunction with others, is restricted by the standards set up by the community to ensure the welfare of the people as a whole.

COMMUNISM

There is a growing number of States where private property and private enterprise do not exist or exist only to a small and limited extent. In the communist States, all property belongs to the State and a central authority controls and directs the factors of production, decides upon the nature and size of production, estimates the wants of the people, and decides which wants shall be satisfied and the means and methods of production to be employed; in short, this authority performs the functions that are carried out under private enterprise by the *price system* where production tends to follow price movements, to rise when prices rise and fall when prices fall.

The *economy is planned*, with the objective of serving the interests of the State as a whole. The needs of the citizens might be sacrificed so that the State might prosper; people might have to do without homes and clothes and the productive mechanism be devoted to producing capital goods such as machines, transport, etc., which will enable the State to become an industrial nation.

No State is completely communist. The Union of Soviet Socialist Republics (U.S.S.R.) began as a group of true communist communities with all workers giving up their produce to the State, but gradually some relaxation was permitted; personal effects are, of course, privately held and now some small private businesses are allowed to operate, while the price system has also had to be introduced.

PLANNING

Economic planning is not confined to communist countries. It is generally regarded as necessary in the so-called emergent countries, the underdeveloped countries that are now trying to stimulate their economic growth. There is, also, a growing amount of planning in capitalist countries where private enterprise prevails. It has been found necessary in many countries to regulate economic conditions.

Britain, France and the United States of America (U.S.A.), for instance, have planned sections of their economies, and in Britain an official planning body, *The National Economic Development Council*, was set up in 1962 to examine the economic performance of the nation, to consider obstacles to economic growth and find ways of stimulating economic growth. The members of the Council are representatives of employers' federations, of the Trades Union Congress, and eminent industrialists, economists and members of the Government. A number of smaller *Economic Development Committees* were set up to investigate conditions in several industries, including machine tool manufacture, motor manufacture, mechanical engineering, wool textiles, rubber, chocolate and sugar confectionery, and exports.

As their enquiries are completed these committees are disbanded.

ECONOMIC LAWS

It is the task of the Economist to examine and classify the complicated workings of the economic system so as to reduce them to some orderly pattern for convenience of study and further investigation. When his researches reveal uniformities of behaviour or action, he is able to formulate *Economic Laws*, which are statements that, given certain causes in the economic sphere, certain effects are likely to follow.

An *economic* law is not like a *statutory* law. It is not a command that must be obeyed under penalty. It is a statement of a *tendency* that can be expected to work out in certain circumstances. As all economic questions involve human action, and as human nature is so variable, the same circumstances might not arise in a given case, and the expected tendency will then not work out. Thus economic laws cannot be rigid or permanent. If *other things are equal*, a certain result can be expected to follow a certain set of conditions; but the conditions may change, other conditions may intervene, and the expected result will not appear.

From his observations, the Economist knows that *other things being equal*, a shortage in the supply of an article causes a rise in its price. Hence, he is able to say that if there is a shortage of food, prices may be expected to rise and only the richer people will be able to get supplies. But other things may not be equal. The Government may fix maximum prices for food and may ration supplies so that the poor and rich have an equal chance of getting what they need. Then the expected rise in price will not take place. This does not mean that the economic law is wrong, but that its working is checked because other things are not equal. In just the same way, the law of gravity is not proved wrong because a balloon goes up in the air.

THE UTILITY OF ECONOMICS

The Economist serves a useful purpose in Society because *his power of prediction*, based on his study and investigation of the economic system, enables him to point out the dangers of a certain line of conduct. As a scientific investigator, he does not approve or disapprove of such conduct; his job is to analyse facts, to explain the working of the economic system, and to point out what will happen if certain lines of conduct are followed. He can show that a war causes economic loss and a wasteful use of economic resources; but as an Economist, he cannot say whether, in any given situation, war is advisable or not. War involves many non-economic issues which are matters for the Statesman and Diplomat, not for the Economist.

The Economist can explain why the wages of skilled engineers are usually high in comparison with the wages of labourers; but the boy leaving school, or his parents, must *choose* whether he is to be a labourer or to become an engineer.

A study of Economics thus serves a useful purpose in modern life. By giving us facts and showing us what may be expected to be the outcome of certain lines of conduct, it helps us to decide which of several alternatives to choose. We ourselves have to make the choice; but our problems are made easier and we can choose more rationally if we know what consequences to expect from our conduct. A study of Economics helps us to choose wisely and avoid many pitfalls in arranging our economic affairs. It enables us to understand how the economic system works and to realise our own position in that system. It also arms us with specialised knowledge which we can use when we have to bring judgment to bear on economic issues, such as an increase in local rates or a rise in the income tax, the imposition of tariffs on imports or the granting of subsidies to certain industries.

CHAPTER II

WANTS: THE MAINSPRING OF EFFORT

THE economic system exists to provide the food, clothes, shelter and other things we require to satisfy our wants. This power or characteristic of satisfying a want is called *utility*.

UTILITY

Utility expresses the relationship between a consumer and a commodity. It implies that the consumer requires the commodity for some purpose or other. But utility is quite distinct from *usefulness*, which implies that something is beneficial. Nuclear missiles cannot be said to be useful; they are harmful to mankind; yet they have utility because they satisfy the want of a belligerent power for a weapon with which to attack and destroy its enemies.

It follows, therefore, that the utility of a commodity varies as between different people. A pacifist has no use for nuclear missiles; meat has no utility for a vegetarian; some people do not like pineapple. Utility also varies at different times. Arms are much more urgently wanted in times of war than in times of peace. People want heating far more in winter than they do in summer.

DIMINISHING UTILITY

The utility of commodities varies also according to the quantity that is available to the consumer. In general, the larger the supply a man has of a thing the less he wants additions to it. In other words, *the utility of additional units of a commodity to any consumer decreases as the consumer's stock of that commodity increases*.

Consider the position of a man in regard to suits of clothes. In a temperate country, he must have some clothing if he is to go out of doors. One suit will have considerable utility. It is possible that another two suits will also have utility; but each extra suit he buys gives him *less satisfaction* than he obtained from the previous suit he bought. He may buy several suits and keep one for day time, one for evening wear, one for golf, one for motoring, one for gardening, and so on. But the more suits he has of any particular kind (*i.e.*, the more evening suits he has, or the more golf suits), the less satisfaction does he get from an additional suit of that kind, until, if he keeps on buying such suits, there comes a time when he would get far more satisfaction by spending the money on something else or even by saving the money.

It is the same with the purchase of any economic good, such as a house, life insurance, food, holidays, shoes and books. There is for each commodity and for every individual a point beyond which the money representing the price of another unit of that commodity could be more advantageously spent on something else. As our desire for a commodity tends to diminish with every increase in the quantity we possess, the utility of each additional unit decreases. This tendency, common to all people and applicable to all things, is expressed by the Economist as the *Law of Diminishing Utility*.

MARGINAL UTILITY

The point at which we buy our last unit of any commodity is known as the *margin*, and the unit we buy at this stage is said to possess *marginal utility*. The total utility of shirts or loaves of bread increases as supply increases; but the larger the supply, the smaller the increase in utility of each *additional* unit.

This brings us to the cardinal rule the consumer

always follows in deciding how much of each commodity he will buy. As the amount of money at his disposal is limited, he will try to distribute it amongst his several purchases in such a way that he cannot gain by spending that amount of money in any other way; he tries, in other words, to derive the greatest possible utility from his expenditure.

To do so, he compares the utilities of the various commodities he wishes to buy. It is of little use comparing the utility of the first loaf of bread he buys per week with the utility of the first packet of chocolate. He knows that he values the bread more highly than the chocolate and if he has to choose between them he will choose the bread; but that does not help him to decide how much of each he will buy. To discover this, he must compare utilities at the margin—the boundary-line—where he starts thinking that he has had enough of one particular commodity for the time being.

The consumer will have solved his problem of deriving maximum satisfaction from his expenditure when the marginal utility of his expenditure on each of his purchases is the same. At this point, he will be indifferent as between various ways of spending his money because a unit of money will give him the same satisfaction whatever he buys. He cannot gain by re-arranging his expenditure in any way. Before this point is reached, he may add to his satisfaction by buying a little more of one thing and a little less of another; if ten pence spent on chocolate gives him greater utility than ten pence spent on bread, he would gain by buying the chocolate. But at the point where marginal utilities are equal, he can add nothing to his satisfaction by re-arranging his expenditure; in other words, he has solved the problem of maximising his satisfaction.

Marginal Utility and Price

The prices of goods and services are not affected by the decisions of a single consumer. The individual consumer finds that prices are already fixed and he must accept those prices in arranging his expenditure. Nor does he pay different prices for different units of a commodity. The fact that the consumer gets decreasing satisfaction from the purchase of each successive packet of chocolate is of no consequence to the shop-keeper—*he charges the same price for each packet*. The buyer will naturally go on buying chocolate as long as the satisfaction he gets from it exceeds the sacrifice (measured by the price) he has to make to pay for it. Obviously, however, there will come a point where the satisfaction from the last chocolate bought just compensates him for parting with the money he has to pay for it. At that point he will not buy any more at the *current price*. But the packet he buys at this point is no better and no worse than the first packet he buys in a week; it is only the relative utility to the consumer that is different. The consumer pays the same price, *i.e.*, the current price, for each packet of chocolate; and the price he pays is a price that is sufficiently low to induce him to purchase the last unit he actually buys. The fact that he buys two packets of chocolate in a week shows that the price per packet is low enough to make the purchase of the second packet worth while. He would buy fewer packets if the price rose, and might buy more if the price fell.

When we are considering whether to spend our money on one thing or on another or whether not to spend it at all, we compare the utility of the two commodities and of the money. Suppose that at a given moment we have fifty pence to spend and that we are undecided whether to buy fish or meat. We cannot afford to buy both, and must, therefore, decide which will give us the greater amount of satisfaction. We, therefore, compare the utility to be derived from spending the money on the fish with the utility we might derive from spending it on meat. In other words, we have to make up our minds which we want the more, and we decide to buy the fish. At the particular moment, therefore, fifty pence spent on fish has greater utility to us than it would have if spent on meat; and it has also greater utility than the money itself, otherwise we would keep our money and do without the fish.

The Paradox of Value

The principle that it is the marginal, and not the total, utility of a commodity that is relevant in connection with the study of prices, supplies the explanation of the so-called "paradox of value". It is a fact that jewels cost far more than most necessaries, but nobody would buy jewels if by so doing he had to go without bread altogether. But this is not the sort of choice that the consumer usually has to make. He does not have to choose between spending £50 on a jewel and going without food; he has to choose between buying a little more of things like food and clothes of which he may already have a lot, and buying a jewel, of which he may not have any. In other words, the buyer of a jewel decides that he will get more satisfaction if he spends an *additional* £50 on jewels rather than on more food and clothing.

Demand

Very few people can be said to have all they want. Most people have to go without some things they would like very much to have; they have to sacrifice some wants. They have a *scale of preferences*; the goods and services they want are listed in their order of preference. The essentials or necessaries of life, the food, clothing, houseroom and medical attention, are high in the scale and, in general, our wants for necessaries cannot be sacrificed; if need be, we are willing to give all our earnings for these essential things. Below the essentials on the scale are the things we need to promote our comfort and raise our standard of living, such as television sets, motor cars and insurance premiums, and low down on the list are non-essentials as, for instance, chocolates, visits to the cinema, that we could well do without if necessary.

In some communities or circumstances a person's earnings may be paid in *kind*; but in modern communities most of us are paid in *money*; and when we wish to obtain things to satisfy our wants, we offer some part of that money in exchange. This offer of money for the satisfaction of our wants constitutes *demand*. Demand may be defined, therefore, as *desire or want, coupled with the willingness and ability to pay for what we want*.

Generally speaking, the greater the utility of an article to us, the more money we are willing to pay for it. But as (according to the Law of Diminishing Utility) later units of a commodity have less utility to us than earlier units, we will ordinarily pay a lower price for each additional unit.

This explains, too, why a greater supply of any commodity can be sold only at a lower price. At a given set of prices, the consumer will have equalised the utilities of his marginal purchases, and at that price he will not wish to buy more of any commodity. But if the price of one commodity falls, he will readjust his expenditure; *e.g.*, if the price of cherries falls, the marginal ten pence spent on cherries will now purchase more than before. The consumer will, therefore, prefer to spend on cherries ten pence he previously spent on ice-cream. Similarly, a rise in the price of cherries will mean that ten pence buys fewer cherries than before; and the consumer will spend his marginal ten pence on something else that will give him greater satisfaction.

This tendency is expressed as the *Law of Demand*. This law states that a fall in price causes demand to rise, while a rise in price causes demand to fall.

INELASTIC AND ELASTIC DEMAND

It will be clear on consideration that this plain statement of the Law of Demand is not always entirely true, that we do not seriously curtail our purchase of such necessaries as bread and milk even if the price rises quite considerably, and that we do not buy much more, if any more, of these commodities even if the price falls. The reason is that we cannot do without these things. Our demand for such essential things is *inelastic*, that is, it *does not change at all, or it changes very little, even with a marked change in price*.

On the other hand, our demand for things that we regard as comforts and luxuries varies to a great extent as their price varies. A moderate fall in the price of television sets or motor cars, for instance, will result in a considerable increase in demand, whereas a rise in their price will have the reverse effect. Many of us buy mushrooms when they are in season and cheap; but most of us have to do without them when they are out of season and their price is high. We increase our consumption of oranges when they become cheap, and at the spring or autumn bargain sales we buy hats, clothes and other things that we might otherwise do without. The demand for these commodities is *elastic*, i.e., *a small rise or fall in price causes a marked change in the amount demanded*.

THE LAW OF SUBSTITUTION

Broadly, then, we say that *the demand for luxuries is elastic and the demand for necessaries inelastic*. But the demand for any given article will be more elastic if there are substitutes for that article. If the price of tea rises, more coffee might be used. This is because we are continually comparing the utility derived from spending money on one commodity with the utility derived from spending the same money on another commodity. And if we find that, by substituting one commodity for another, we can increase our total satisfaction, we unhesitatingly do so. We buy coffee instead of tea; we go to the cinema instead of the theatre; we spend our holidays in Cornwall instead of going to the South of France.

In general, therefore, *we distribute our expenditure so as to obtain the greatest satisfaction from our outlay*, so that the last or marginal pound, or whatever unit of money we choose to take, spent on each commodity gives us an equal measure of satisfaction.

This tendency the Economist sums up as the *Law of Substitution* or *the Law of Equi-Marginal Returns*, which states that our expenditure on different commodities is so distributed that the utilities obtained from the last unit of money spent in each form of consumption are equal. Under the influence of this law, we seek to attain such a position with regard to the various commodities we purchase that there would be no advantage in "switching", say in buying a poundsworth more of this and a poundsworth less of that. We seek the position where we have achieved the most satisfactory allocation of the resources that we apply to satisfying our wants.

CHAPTER III

THE SATISFACTION OF OUR WANTS

In its endless effort to satisfy our wants, the economic community is engaged in making available and in converting the various forms of *natural resources* for our use. The soil is cultivated, cattle are reared, coal is mined, iron is converted into ships and engines, fibres are turned into clothes, the connecting services of transport and of markets are organised, and a thousand and one things are done to supply "goods" and services for the use of those of us who can pay for them.

All these activities, whose purpose is the satisfaction of human wants, constitute *production*, and they result in supplies of (*a*) CONSUMERS' GOODS (*e.g.*, bread, milk, houses), and *various forms of personal service* (*e.g.*, medical and dental services), that satisfy wants *directly*, as well as of (*b*) PRODUCERS' GOODS (such as machinery and tools) and *commercial services* (*e.g.*, insurance), that satisfy wants *indirectly*.

PRODUCTION CREATES UTILITIES

As production exists to satisfy wants, it follows that it results in the *creation of utilities*. Man cannot create matter, but he can alter its form or shape so that it has greater utility; or he can move it from one place (*e.g.*, a coal mine) to another where it has greater utility (*e.g.*, a factory); or he can make it available at a time when it is most required (*e.g.*, ice on a hot summer's day). The farmer does not create matter when he produces a crop of wheat or of cotton. What he does is to place seed in a position favourable for the action of the forces of Nature; by his work with the soil and the seed he creates utilities.

People who produce *services* that directly or indirectly satisfy our wants are just as much producers in the economic sense as people who actually turn out material goods. Those services are an essential part of the modern economic system; without them it could not function as effectively or as efficiently. Hence the banker and barrister, teacher and doctor, lawyer and dustman are just as much producers as the baker, the carpenter and the cotton spinner.

THE FACTORS OF PRODUCTION

Production may be very simple. An inhabitant of the tropics may satisfy his hunger by stretching up his arm and plucking a banana off a tree. He is able to satisfy his need for food with very little effort by using a free gift of Nature. But the tin of salmon that we buy for our evening meal involves a much more complex system of production. Much involved production and administrative machinery, much more effort of brain and body, and more gifts of Nature have to be combined to satisfy this apparently simple want. The salmon and the material from which the container is made are provided by Nature. But the fish has to be caught and brought to the canneries; the iron and tin have to be mined, transported and transformed into the container; machinery is required to make the necessary transformation; marketing organisation and transport are necessary to bring the tin and its contents to the consumer; and above all, there must be a controlling and directing authority to set in motion and direct all the machinery and people employed.

If we examine the various agencies involved in the production of any such product, we find that they can be divided into three groups, which the Economist calls the *Factors of Production*, viz., *land*, *labour* and *capital*. Simple production involves the use of two of these factors only, land and labour; complex production—and almost all production nowadays is complex—involves the use of all the factors, and also of a co-ordinating factor that sets the other factors in motion, controls and directs them and keeps them working efficiently and profitably. This factor is *enterprise*.

LAND OR NATURAL RESOURCES

The Economist uses the term "land" to mean not only land itself as a space whereon we can build a house or a factory, but also *everything that is provided by Nature*, *i.e.*, all *natural resources* such as the natural properties of the soil, mineral deposits, vegetation, fish, animals, sunlight, wind and water. Actually, everything that we require to satisfy our needs is dependent ultimately on Nature, though she has to be assisted in various ways before we can take advantage of her bounty.

Rich virgin soil will at first provide an abundance of crops in return for very little effort. With relatively little labour and expense, it can be cultivated to provide plentiful supplies of food. But Nature's bounty is not unlimited; she is generous only up to a point. Beyond that she becomes niggardly and it becomes more and more costly to wrest away her treasures. After a time, man finds that a given outlay of work and money yields only a *diminishing return*. Repeated applications of manure to the same plot of land give decreasing results, and the same thing happens if more and more men are employed on the same farm. In coal-mining, decreasing results are obtained from a unit of money spent, as shafts have to be sunk still deeper and the coal-face extended still farther. The deeper we have to go for coal, the farther afield we have to go for oil or gold, the wider the waters we have to search for a profitable catch, the less the return to our labour.

The Law of Diminishing Returns

This tendency of Nature is expressed in one of the most vital laws of Economics, the *Law of Diminishing Returns*. Applied to land, the law states that *an increase in the capital and labour applied in the cultivation of land causes* IN GENERAL a *less than proportionate increase in the amount of produce raised*.

Briefly, this law means that, after a point, costs of production on a given plot of land tend to increase at a higher rate than output. A farmer cultivating the same area of land is bound to find ultimately that the return to every application of labour and capital to a given amount of land is lower than the return to previous applications, and at last there comes a point where it does not pay him to apply to that land any more capital and labour. At this point the return or reward he receives from the last application just compensates him for his outlay on wages and materials. To incur further expenditure would merely involve him in loss. This point, where it is not worth his while to apply any more capital and labour to a given piece of land, is known as the *margin of cultivation*.

Although the Law of Diminishing Returns operates at a relatively early stage in agriculture and in other extractive industries (*e.g.*, mining and fishing), it must operate ultimately in all industries. In manufacturing industries, the operation of the Law of Diminishing Returns can be postponed for a time by man's inventiveness and resourcefulness, but, ultimately, natural and human factors cause the rate of return to diminish. As applied generally, the law states that whenever a variable factor of production is used in combination with a constant factor, returns to additional units of expenditure at first increase more than in proportion to the additional applications of the varying factor, but a point is reached when the returns begin to increase less than in proportion. In manufacture, the constant factor is management.

MALTHUS'S GLOOMY DOCTRINE

It follows from the Law of Diminishing Returns that, as population increases and the demands on natural resources are intensified, man's wants can be satisfied only at an ever-increasing cost. This possibility was first investigated very many years ago by *Thomas Malthus*,[1] who contended that the *natural tendency of a thriving people was to increase at a higher rate than the increase in the means of subsistence*, with the result that, if population was not deliberately restrained by a low birthrate, Nature would provide her own remedy and population would be reduced by a high death-rate, caused by disease, war or starvation.

Fortunately, Malthus's forebodings have not been realised. The operation of the Law of Diminishing Returns has been delayed by inventions, *e.g.*, of machinery and of new techniques and fertilisers, and by greater production from improved seed and from new varieties of crops, while the desire for a higher standard of living has in many countries led to a decline in the birth-rate.

At the same time, it is generally recognised that there is in respect of any country an *optimum size of population*, *i.e.*, a population of such a size or density that an increase or a decrease, with the existing methods of production, will lead to a smaller output per head. At this "optimum size", a population can best be supplied with the things it needs, and this size, therefore, is that at which a community ought to aim. The difficulty, of course, is that there is no satisfactory method of judging what is the optimum, or best, size of population at any time in any particular country.

[1] Malthus's *Essay on Population*, first published in 1798.

Labour

Labour *includes all manual and mental effort undertaken for a reward*. The effort exerted by the professional footballer is labour because it is undertaken *for a wage*; but the effort of the *amateur* player, even though it may far exceed that of the professional, is not regarded as labour from the economic point of view. The services of a nurse who receives payment are regarded as labour, but the services of a mother who cares for her sick child are not so regarded. The services in both cases may be equally useful and beneficial, but work and service undertaken out of love and affection are not the subject of economic study. The Economist is concerned with one kind of labour only, *i.e.*, *labour that receives a reward measurable in terms of money*.

Labour produces either goods or services. At one time only labour employed in the production of goods was regarded as *productive*, and labour that produced services (*e.g.*, the labour of the professional player or paid singer) was regarded as *unproductive*.

Nowadays, Economists make no such distinction. They regard the services of the farmer, transport worker, weaver, clerk, banker, doctor, soldier, sailor, policeman and nurse as productive because their services have a value and that value is *measurable in terms of money*. This economic conception of labour does not imply that the Economist is a stony-hearted philosopher who ignores *unpaid* services because he thinks they are of no use. On the contrary, he realises that they are necessary to human welfare and may be very beneficial in promoting efficiency. But the Economist is a scientist, and, as such, he must deal with things that can be measured by some standard or measuring rod. To him, money is that standard.

CAPITAL

"Capital" refers to all material resources, other than land and labour, that are used in production. Capital exists only as the result of the co-operation of labour and natural resources. In the most primitive community, capital does not exist. But as soon as man, having applied his labour to natural resources, is able to set aside a supply of potatoes or of wheat for seed for the future, and to fashion tools, however crude, to assist him in future production, he is accumulating capital. Capital, therefore, is the *produced* agent of production.

A very simple example of capital is the needle used to make an article of clothing. The needle helps to produce something else, in this case a finished garment. In principle, therefore, a needle is just as much capital as the biggest and most complicated machine, because both have been produced to help to produce other things. Capital, in fact, includes all "producers' goods", such as machinery, plant, tools and raw materials that are used in production, as well as such things as railways, canals, docks and roads that constitute the fixed capital of the nation.

Land and labour are both far more efficient and productive when used in combination with adequate supplies of capital. Moreover, all production takes time, and in the case of practically all commodities there is a waiting period before the commodity is ready for marketing and for consumption. During this waiting period all those engaged in production (workers and employers) have to be supported, and it is the function of capital, in addition to supplying the necessary appliances and materials, to provide this support. *Capital, accumulated in the past, is applied to finance production for the future.*

There is only one way of accumulating capital, and that is by *saving* some part of that which is produced, *i.e.*, by putting aside for future use some part of what we are producing now. The farmer accumulates capital when he retains part of his crop to use as seed; the manufacturer accumulates capital when he builds up a reserve for future extensions of his premises and plant.

The man who lives from hand to mouth can save nothing except a part of his *time*. But even then he can accumulate capital by devoting less time to leisure or to producing goods for his immediate consumption, and by using the time so saved in making tools that will facilitate his efforts to satisfy his wants. If a person can avoid living from hand to mouth, he can set aside, *i.e.*, *save*, part of his produce and use it to sustain himself during the period he devotes to making tools, machinery and other aids to production.

The accumulation of capital depends, therefore, on labour and saving. In modern times the saving is actually done in terms of money; people who have a surplus they do not wish to use for purchasing goods for immediate consumption either use the surplus themselves, or they lend it to others, for creating producers' goods. In general, money is invested in stocks or shares or placed in bank deposits, whence it ultimately finds its way into such producers' goods as machinery, plant, factories, railways and raw materials.

Enterprise: The Entrepreneur

So that the goods we need shall be available at the time when and the place where we need them, some coordinating and controlling authority is required to bring the various factors of production together in the necessary proportions, to make their efforts efficient, to see that each is properly rewarded, to decide on the nature, quality and quantity of the product, to arrange for the marketing and distribution of the output, and to bear the whole risk of the success or failure of the enterprise.

These functions of co-ordinating, controlling and assuming the risk of business are performed by a person whom the Economist describes as the *entrepreneur* (French = "undertaker"), though in business he may be known as the proprietor or owner or partner.

The entrepreneur is the person who is responsible for initiating and organising the business, for the "enterprise" behind the concern, and also for *bearing the risk* or uncertainty that cannot be separated from any undertaking. In performing the threefold functions of *developing the idea*, of *co-ordinating and controlling* the business and of *assuming the risk* of production, the entrepreneur seeks to keep costs low and efficiency high. He acts as the link between the unorganised consumer and the unorganised factors of production, viz., money, capital goods, man-power and raw materials; and he takes the risk that the things he produces will not meet the requirements of the consumer.

Actually, the consumer does not always decide for himself what he wants. He is often induced by advertising and in other ways to buy things that he scarcely realises he needs. Hence we frequently find to-day that, although all production is undertaken in order to satisfy demand, demand is often created by those who have the means, the ability and the organisation to put a given product on the market. Thus the entrepreneur, having decided what to produce, is largely concerned with bringing to the public notice the nature and advantages of his product, so that it can be sold at a price that will cover cost and provide a profit, the size of the profit depending on his success in bearing the risk.

As modern industrial organisation is so complex, this function of initiating and organising production is clearly of the utmost importance. The efficiency of the other three factors of production may easily be impaired or the factors themselves rendered useless by lack of directive ability.

In this task of co-ordinating the other three factors that he uses, and of controlling the production and marketing of his product, the entrepreneur is really discharging only a specialised form of labour, for which, of course, he receives a salary or wage that is commensurate with the skill he has to display. The entrepreneur's essential function of bearing the risk involved in production is, however, something quite different from labour or organisation or management, and is different also from the services provided by the other factors.

RISK-BEARING

In the complex economic system, where production is largely initiated ahead of demand and must be based on estimates of the future, risks are unavoidable. The manufacturer of a new model motor-car must make his plans months before the first car is sold, and when his factories are equipped, his staff assembled and his machines ready to run, he has to make up his mind how many cars he will turn out. His new model may prove an enormous success, in which case he must be ready to handle orders very quickly, or competitors will jump in and his business will suffer. On the other hand, the new car may prove an absolute failure, in which case immediate action must be taken to improve it or to curtail the plans for its production.

Whatever the event, it is the entrepreneur's job to decide well in advance, and his reputation as well as his success depend on the foresight, judgment and courage with which he makes his plans and estimates. Clearly, the development of new products and the marketing of new inventions depend almost entirely on the capacity and willingness of men to undertake pioneer work and to shoulder risks, and unless such men are given great scope and enticed by the possibilities of high rewards, it will not be worth their while to face the trouble and risk of starting a business.

The bearing of risk is, therefore, regarded as a separate factor of production, quite distinct from the other factors. It is the one function associated with the entrepreneur that cannot be passed on to hired assistants. Whilst the function of management, for example, can be passed on to one or a number of paid managers, risk bearing must be undertaken by the entrepreneur himself, and it, therefore, earns a specific reward—*profit*—the nature and determination of which are considered in Chapter XII.

CHAPTER IV

THE ORGANISATION OF PRODUCTION

BRITAIN'S INDUSTRIES

Agriculture is a very important industry in Britain and employs large numbers of workers but it is not the largest industry. Most of the people live in urban areas, earning their livings in factories, workshops, mines, transport, offices, shops, etc.; they are employed in industries that actually *make* goods or are connected with those industries that make goods. Broadly, the occupations in which men engage for the purpose of earning their livings can be classified in three main groups:

1. *Primary*: These are the industries concerned with *growing* things, such as crops and other agricultural products, with raising animals, and *extracting* things from the earth, such as coal and minerals, fish from the sea and trees from the forests, etc.

2. *Secondary*: These are the industries that *make* things, converting them from raw materials and semi-manufactured goods into finished products; for instance, the manufacture of material goods, such as clothes, furniture, ships and locomotives, and the building of houses, roads and bridges.

3. *Tertiary*: These are services; *commercial* services further the progress of goods from producer to consumer and include transport, banking and insurance services; *professional* services, such as are provided by the legal, accountancy, medical and teaching professions, are given direct to the consumer.

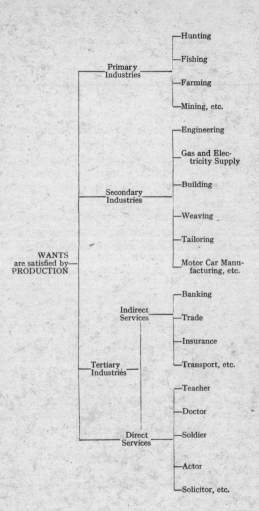

WANTS
are satisfied by—
PRODUCTION

Primary Industries
- Hunting
- Fishing
- Farming
- Mining, etc.

Secondary Industries
- Engineering
- Gas and Electricity Supply
- Building
- Weaving
- Tailoring
- Motor Car Manufacturing, etc.

Tertiary Industries

Indirect Services
- Banking
- Trade
- Insurance
- Transport, etc.

Direct Services
- Teacher
- Doctor
- Soldier
- Actor
- Solicitor, etc.

A man may earn his living by working for himself; he may be a *one-man concern*, he alone providing all the factors of production and carrying through the business in all its aspects. One-man businesses are not very frequent though they persist where the consumer requires personal and individual attention, as in bespoke tailoring, and in general medical practitioners' service, though even in such cases, *partnerships* may be more suitable, allowing for division of labour and the combination of the different aptitudes of the partners, and for more capital if it is needed.

The dominant form of business enterprise to-day is the *public company*. It has large capital, supplied by shareholders of various kinds—preference and ordinary shareholders—and by debenture-holders.

Public corporations also employ large numbers of people. They are the concerns that are responsible for controlling and running the nationalised industries such as the electricity, gas, coal and railway systems in Britain.

Co-operative societies in the retail trade are also expanding in Britain. In this type of organisation, the members are the owners of the stores.

THE DIVISION OF LABOUR

The producing and selling of goods are organised differently in different conditions of society. At one time production was very simple. One man produced one article. Each community had its tinker, tailor, baker, blacksmith, cobbler and carpenter, each a specialist in his own craft, devoting his whole time to his job, making an article from start to finish, and relying on other specialists for such other goods as he required.

This system still prevails in some less advanced communities, but in most modern communities the productive organisation is far more complex. Nowadays a worker may specialise in producing only a very small part of the ultimate product. He may, in fact, never see the finished article, and in the great majority of cases he will never use it. The man who helps to make a suit of clothes in a large ready-made tailoring firm may never see the complete suit of which his work forms a part; the worker who makes wireless valves may never handle the instruments in which those valves are ultimately used.

This system, whereby a man does one specialised job instead of many different jobs and numerous men work on different sections of the ultimate product, is known as the "division of labour". We find the simplest form of division of labour when two men get together to tackle the same job; as when two men carry a log too heavy for one to carry, or when one of two fishermen rows the boat whilst the other handles the rods and lines.

In most cases to-day, however, the division of labour is much more complex. The majority of modern industrial products involve a large number of different processes and an army of specialised workers, most of whom are engaged in making only a small part of the ultimate product. In the making of a shirt, for example, one man cuts out the shirt, usually with a cutting machine, another machines the long seams, another makes the sleeves, another makes the buttonholes (usually with a machine), while still another puts on the buttons (again by machine). Some shirts are made entirely by hand, but the majority of men have to be content with a cheaper, machine-made product, which, of course, serves the same purpose, though it has not the same appeal to the fastidious.

Apart from such specialisation within an industry, there is specialisation also between industries, and even between countries. The production of the cotton from which shirts are made involves the co-operation of many industries, such as cotton-growing, cotton-ginning, cotton-spinning, cotton-weaving, bleaching, finishing, wholesaling, retailing and transportation. Each of these is a specialised branch contributing its quota of work and material to the ultimate product.

Even in the making of such an apparently simple thing as a shirt, two, three or more countries may be involved. The country that produces the cotton may not be the same as that which manufactures the shirt; whilst the country that undertakes the manufacture may have to get the necessary specialised machinery from one country, and the coal that drives the machinery from yet another.

Again, tropical countries do not usually develop heavy steel industries. Anything they require in this line, such as parts of bridges and railways, can be obtained more cheaply from temperate countries, rich in minerals, which in turn require the fruits and other products of the tropical country that they themselves cannot grow or can grow only at very great expense. By such specialisation, the people of each of the countries apply themselves to the tasks for which they are best fitted, and there is a resulting all-round advantage.

EFFECTS OF THE DIVISION OF LABOUR

The general effect of the division of labour is that each worker specialises in doing one particular job, and thereby becomes more efficient. The aptitudes of different men for different tasks are utilised as fully as possible.

A worker who specialises on one process has less to learn and consequently becomes more quickly proficient than if he had to learn all the processes involved in the making of one article. He saves time not only in learning his trade, but also, as he becomes more proficient, in doing his job and in not constantly changing from one set of tools to another. There is also an economy in the use of tools; a specialist can use his tools more continuously and carefully than a man who has to use several sets of tools. Again, the workman who is continuously doing the same job gets to know much more about it than a man who does several jobs. Thus division of labour leads to a specialised, keener knowledge of each process and part process, with the general result that a larger output can be produced at less cost per article, and that the quality of the product, each part of which is made by a specialist, is superior.

As the breaking up of production into separate jobs or processes tends to reduce the task of each worker to a mechanical routine, it makes more easily possible the invention of machinery and its use as a substitute for labour. In some directions this may not be an advantage, as, for example, when skilled workers are reduced to semi-skilled machine tenders. On the other hand, the use of machinery frequently increases man's command over Nature and relieves the worker of much drudgery and wearisome toil. Man to-day can perform tasks which were formerly either impossible or would have taken ages to complete. The Forth Bridge might conceivably have been built by manpower alone, but the cost and the time taken would have been enormous.

DISADVANTAGES OF THE DIVISION OF LABOUR

To the worker the chief disadvantage of the division of labour is that efficiency is obtained at the expense of the worker's personality. When work is sub-divided into a large number of small operations, it inevitably becomes uninteresting and monotonous. The worker finds little scope for his creative instinct, loses a sense of pride in his work, exercises very little initiative and undertakes little responsibility. The man who spends his life tightening nuts on car chassis in a motor-car factory cannot be expected to have much pride or interest in the ultimate product; as long as his nuts are properly tightened he is not concerned whether the cars will run or not.

It is sometimes found, too, that highly specialised labour is relatively *immobile*: *it does not move easily to a different type of work*. The man who has spent years doing one small job cannot turn his hand to something else as easily as a man who has performed a variety of operations. As a result, workers may find difficulty in moving to another industry when their own is depressed.

The Law of Increasing Returns

On the whole, however, machinery satisfies man's ever-increasing desire for more and better goods, and modern manufacturing methods generally enable him to get what he wants at a relatively decreasing cost per unit.

Costs per unit fall mainly because every manufacturer, in the pursuit of self-interest, continues to extend the scale of his operations so long as he obtains a more than proportionate return from his employment of labour and capital. Suppose, for example, that a manufacturer can turn out 5,000 articles for an expenditure of £1,000 and that, by spending an extra £100 on labour or on plant, he can increase his output to 5,600 articles. Clearly, the manufacturer will not hesitate to spend the £100, because it enables him to reduce his cost per unit of output, *i.e.*, to increase his returns more than proportionately to the extra outlay. And he will continue to increase his expenditure so long as he can be certain of the increased return. In fact, throughout all manufacturing industry there is a tendency in this direction, because manufacturing industry is subject to the *Law of Increasing Returns*, viz., that, *up to a point, the expansion of an industry by additions of labour and capital tends to be accompanied by a more than proportionate increase in the returns*.

Increasing returns tend to be obtained in manufacture because, until a factory organisation is working at full capacity—until every machine is being worked to the full, every inch of space taken up, the heating and lighting system used with the utmost economy, all supervisors and managers fully and efficiently employed—every expansion of output means that the *fixed* or *supplementary costs* (*i.e.*, the costs that do not vary with output, such as rent and rates, debenture interest and administrative salaries) are spread over a larger number of units of output, so that the cost of production of each unit is less. It costs a printer very little more to turn out 5,000 leaflets than 1,000, for once the type is set up, the only additional cost is that of paper, ink and of running the machine. The printer's rent, rates and machinery costs, as well as the original cost of type-setting, are spread over a much larger number of units, and the greater the number of units the less the cost per unit.

In every manufacturing business, however, there comes a time when the machinery and the productive organisation reach their most efficient limit and are being worked to full capacity. Usually the limit is reached because of the failure of the human element; a point is reached when the strain on the management becomes too severe and it cannot keep pace with the expansion of the other factors, *i.e.*, it cannot efficiently co-ordinate the business when it extends beyond a certain size. As a result, any increase in output beyond this point of *optimum size* is possible only at an increased cost per article because the Law of Diminishing Returns begins to operate.

The Localisation of Industry

There is a tendency for industries to be carried on, not only by specialists who are most capable of making them pay, but also in those regions which are most suited to them and where they are most likely to be profitable. The manufacture of woollen goods is associated with Yorkshire, of pottery with Staffordshire, of linen with Belfast, of cutlery and steel with Sheffield.

Originally, industries were set up in particular regions because of the presence of local supplies of essential raw materials or of water power or of coal. The wool from the sheep of the Yorkshire Moors was largely responsible for the growth of the Yorkshire woollen industry; Staffordshire pottery owes its origin to local clay and coal; Belfast linen to local supplies of flax, and so on. But as a result of the growth and cheapness of transport, and the large-scale production of raw materials in the newer countries, this kind of "pull" is no longer as strong as it was. Now many industries, including the woollen industry of Yorkshire, are situated thousands of miles from the sources of the raw materials on which they depend. For the same reasons nearness to markets is not as important as once it was. Transport facilities make it possible to send goods over long distances with comparative speed, cheapness and safety. Hence, Yorkshire, which at one time produced mainly for the home market, now sends her worsteds and her woollens to other parts of the world.

Following the *Industrial Revolution*, the term applied to the period roughly between 1760 and 1850, when the processes of industry were revolutionised by the use of steam for power and by many other important scientific discoveries and inventions, factories tended to be established near the source of power, then chiefly coal. As a result several of Britain's most prosperous industries developed on the coal-fields, because it was cheaper to take the raw material to the fuel than to take the heavy and bulky fuel to the raw material. With the increasing use of electricity and oil, the attractive power of the coal-fields became far less marked. To-day the tendency is for industries to become widely scattered and, in choosing industrial sites, regard may be paid to a variety of considerations, such as nearness to markets, pleasurable and healthy surroundings, adequate labour supply, low local rates, as well as to other forms of power such as electricity.

A region that has specialised in a certain industry or industries tends to attract other firms in the same industries because there are many common advantages that all can enjoy. Generations of skilled workmen are brought up in the trade, so there is always a supply of skilled labour available; transport and communications become adapted to the particular needs of the industry; there are organised markets for buying materials and disposing of the finished products; subsidiary industries spring up that absorb the by-products of the major industry; organisations, institutions and associations peculiar to the industry are established in the neighbourhood and afford facilities that are too valuable to be ignored.

The business man's choice of the district where he will begin operations is, therefore, somewhat limited if his industry is one that is strongly localised in a given area, as, for example, the woollen industry of Yorkshire. If he seeks to operate elsewhere, he might find he is at a disadvantage as compared with his competitors. But if he is not forced to consider any such factor, he will choose a site that offers the maximum net advantages for his particular business.

The localisation of industries in certain regions which became centres of heavy population, with most of the members of a family employed in the same industry, had unfortunate effects in periods of depression. In the great depression of the 1930's, in those parts of Lancashire, Yorkshire, South Wales and Scotland where the heavy industries had flourished around the coal-fields, there was very heavy unemployment and the consequent distress of whole families persisted for many years. These declining industries had been the main sources of British exports before the First World War, and when overseas markets were lost during the war, never to be regained, a large number of workers became unemployed, with little hope of finding jobs in those areas or in those industries.

To avoid a repetition of these conditions and achieve a better balanced distribution of industries, the Government has introduced measures to *control the location of industries*. The areas of heavy unemployment were designated "depressed" areas and given special Government assistance. Later they became "special" areas, and now they are "development" districts, receiving concessions and financial assistance to induce new factories and new industries to settle there, the object being to take "work to the workers", rather than to make it necessary for workers and their families to uproot themselves and start life anew in strange surroundings. The *New Towns Act*, 1946, provided for the building of several new towns to take some of the people and industries away from London and other large towns and of other new towns near to the old towns where the people could continue to work at their jobs.

THE SIZE OF THE BUSINESS

When we survey the field of man's activities, we see that in some industries the typical firm or *business unit* is small, as in agriculture in Britain, where the small farm employing a few labourers is the most common unit. In others, as, for example, the steel industry, the business firm is large, as is shown by the fact that the majority of workers in the steel industry are employed in plants that employ over 500 workers each.

What, then, are the factors that determine the size that a business ultimately attains? On examination we find that there are three mains factors: (*a*) the nature of the industry, whether manufacturing or extractive; (*b*) the nature of the product; and (*c*) the nature of the demand for the product.

In agriculture and other extractive industries, the typical unit is small because the limit to increasing returns is soon reached, *i.e.*, diminishing returns begin to operate at an early stage, and expansion into a very large unit would in general not be profitable. In most manufacturing industries, however, the typical unit is large because of the *economies of scale, i.e.*, the *internal and external economies* that emerge when the amount of all factors used in production is increased. These economies are available at a larger scale but not at the smaller scale; in brief, production on a large scale is more economical than at a smaller scale.

The size of the business unit also varies according to the nature of the product. In general it is large where the technique of the industry necessitates large fixed capital, *i.e.*, extensive plant and heavy machinery (as in the case of shipbuilding and locomotive building); or where much of the work can be reduced to routine, *e.g.*, cigarette manufacture; or where the product can be standardised, as in the motor-car industry. In such circumstances, substantial advantages accrue to large-scale operations.

There are, however, certain manufacturing industries where the typical unit tends to be small. These are industries in which the product cannot be standardised and the nature of the demand makes a wide variety of design and material essential, as, for example, the furniture industry and the printing industry, or industries catering for a small irregular or fashionable demand, as, for example, various artistic and luxury trades, such as those producing high-class ladies' dresses, hats and shoes.

Where demand is large and constant, and not subject to changes in fashion, as in the case of soap, buckets and other household utensils in everyday use, the typical producing firm is large; but it is small in businesses where close attention must be paid to the whims of the consumer, as in many branches of the retail trade, *e.g.*, high-class bespoke tailoring, and in the professions, *e.g.*, the legal and medical services.

LARGE-SCALE PRODUCTION

While the small unit thus persists in various branches of business and industry, large-scale production is the typical feature of modern industrial organisation. If a producer can work on a large scale he will do so, because he has then more scope for obtaining the advantages of increasing returns and of the division of labour. Standing charges are spread over a larger number of units of the product, and plant, machinery, tools and materials are used more economically. By-products may be turned to profitable use by the firm as well as by subsidiary industries. Expensive research and experiment can be afforded, and the large firm has better opportunities for advertising and publicity than its smaller rival.

This may be summarised by the statement that the larger firm obtains more benefit than its smaller rival from *internal and external economies of production*.

From the point of view of production, large-scale organisation has, in fact, few disadvantages, and these arise mainly from the difficulty of control. Large businesses tend to become unwieldy. Also, a large organisation cannot quickly and easily change the direction of its effort or the nature of its product if circumstances arise that make such a change necessary. A large-scale firm that is organised to produce a special type of motor-car for a foreign market cannot switch its plant over to the manufacture of something else if its market is suddenly closed because of the outbreak of war, or because of the application of import restrictions. Sometimes, too, the concentration of direction in a few hands lends itself to abuse, which not infrequently operates to the detriment of the consumer, as when he gets an inferior article or has to pay too high a price. It is largely because the small firm does not suffer from these disadvantages that it can still hold its own in the struggle for economic existence.

CHAPTER V

THE COST OF SATISFYING WANTS

We have seen that the demand for goods stimulates their production and that productive activity, carried out under widely differing conditions, results in the supply of all kinds of goods available for consumption. We have now to discover what determines the *extent* of the supply of different kinds of goods. We know that there is not always on the market a sufficient supply of a certain commodity to satisfy the whole of the demand for it. It is not always possible to buy a lettuce or a pound of good tomatoes, even when they are in season. What are the factors, then, that bring goods to market? How does the farmer or manufacturer decide *how much* of a given commodity to produce at any given time?

The Law of Supply

By supply we mean the quantity of a commodity that is *actually offered for sale at any particular time*, as distinguished from the *stock* of the commodity that is in existence at that particular time. In the case of perishable articles, stock and supply tend to coincide, for such articles cannot be kept back from the market except for a comparatively short period. On the other hand, the supply of commodities of a lasting nature, such as the precious metals and precious stones, is usually but a small proportion of the total amount available.

According to the *Law of Supply*, a rise in price tends to increase supply and a fall in price tends to reduce it. If over a period the price of wheat gradually rises, farmers will increase their production of wheat in order to take advantage of the increased price. On the other hand, if the world price of crude rubber falls considerably, the plantation producers restrict their output and some of them may go out of business altogether.

ELASTICITY OF SUPPLY

Although the supply of a commodity brought to the market thus depends on the market price, the supply of some commodities can be far more quickly adjusted to changes in price than the supply of other commodities, and the degree of readiness with which supply can be thus adjusted to a change in price depends on what is called the *elasticity* of the supply.

When the supply of a commodity can be readily adjusted to changes in price the supply of that commodity is said to be *elastic*, as is the case with the supply of most manufactured goods in general use, *e.g.*, moderately priced household furniture, household requisites such as soap, and domestic utensils such as dust-bins and buckets. The supply of such articles can be quickly increased or reduced to meet changes in price.

When the supply of a commodity cannot be readily adjusted to meet changes in price, it is said to be *inelastic*, as is the case with wheat, rubber, cattle and other things that have to be cultivated or grown or reared. In general, a prolonged rise in the price of one of these commodities will lead to an increase in the supply; but that increase does not come about immediately because it takes some time for producers to decide to increase their outputs and, even when they have done so, it takes a long time for the additional supplies to be ready for the market. The supply of manufactured goods that take a long time to plan and to produce, such as ships, locomotives and other large machines, is also inelastic.

Whether the supply of a commodity is inelastic or elastic, a producer will be willing to increase his supplies of that commodity only if he believes that he can obtain such a price for his total output as will cover his *costs of production*.

COSTS OF PRODUCTION

Costs of production arise in all types of business, agricultural, extractive or manufacturing; in businesses or professions concerned with the production of services as well as in businesses that produce material goods. By way of illustration, however, let us consider the costs of a man who starts a manufacturing business. Having first of all bought or rented a site, he has to build a factory and equip it with plant, machinery, heating and lighting; he must engage workers of all kinds—skilled, unskilled, clerical and perhaps research; and then he has to buy such raw materials and power as are needed.

The manufacturer must pay for all such things, in most cases long before his product is anything like ready for market, and the total expenses in which he is thus involved constitute his "costs of production". Usually, these costs are divided into two sections called (1) *variable* or *prime* costs, and (2) *fixed* or *supplementary* costs, or, as they are sometimes called, *overhead* costs.

VARIABLE COSTS are costs that vary with output. A boot manufacturer may have a factory and machines that can produce from 10,000 to 30,000 pairs of boots. Whichever quantity he produces, the plant and factory will cost just the same; but if he decides to produce the larger quantity, there will be a considerable increase in the total costs because more leather, more fuel, more lighting and probably more labour will be required. These expenses that rise or fall with changes in output constitute the manufacturer's "prime" costs.

FIXED or SUPPLEMENTARY COSTS are charges that do not change as output is increased or decreased. So long as the boot manufacturer does not change or extend his factory, his rent is the same whatever his output; whether he is producing little or much, he has to pay that rent, and it is the same with rates, insurance premiums and interest on any original capital he may have borrowed. Moreover, his allowance for depreciation of his machinery and premises must be made at the same rate whether his output is large or small. All such overhead charges vary little whether the factory is working full time or not, but *variable costs stop when the factory stops*.

From the Economist's standpoint, a producer's total costs of production include a *normal* profit, over and above an allowance for interest on the producer's own capital. The figure of profit which a manufacturer considers reasonable in view of the risk he runs in producing for an uncertain future demand may, therefore, be regarded as a "supplementary" cost.

In the long run, a manufacturer's sales-receipts must cover his variable and his fixed costs, including a reasonable or normal profit, or he will leave the business. For a short period he might continue to produce even though he does not cover all his costs, *i.e.*, he might run at a loss, but he will do his utmost to cover at least his variable costs. In a period of depression, for instance, the manufacturer may continue to produce and to keep his plant, labour, etc., occupied so long as his variable costs are covered, and if he can make some contribution towards his fixed costs, so much the better for him. Hoping for better days, he is reluctant to close his factory, or to sell his plant, perhaps at a heavy loss. And when the better days do come, he tries to make up for the absence of profit during the slack period by producing as much as he profitably can.

MARGINAL COST OF PRODUCTION

Over bad times and good, *i.e.*, *in the long run*, every producer must cover what are known as *marginal costs*, *i.e.*, the costs of the marginal unit of his output. This is the unit that he finds it least profitable to produce.

Marginal cost of production performs the same function in influencing price from the side of supply as does marginal utility on the side of demand. We have seen that the price a consumer is willing to give for a unit of a given supply of a commodity tends to equal the marginal utility of that supply, *i.e.*, the utility of the unit that is least urgently required. But we must also know at what price the producer of that commodity will be willing to part with the goods he supplies. A symmetrical influence on price is, therefore, the marginal cost of that supply, *i.e.*, *the cost of adding another unit to the supply*.

Goods are supplied to the market by producers of varying efficiency. Some, perhaps owing to lack of modern equipment, but not necessarily to lack of competent management, can just keep their heads above water. Such firms are known as *"marginal producers"*, and they remain in business because their contribution to the total supply raises that supply to the level required to satisfy demand.

At that level of demand, the price will be just sufficient to enable the marginal firm to continue in production. In other words, price will be just high enough to cover that firm's *average costs*, *i.e.*, total expenses of production (including a minimum profit), divided by the number of commodities produced.

Other firms, however, are more efficient, though they differ in degrees of efficiency. Some make average profits, others exceptional ones, but all firms tend to expand output to the point where marginal cost equals price. While marginal cost, *i.e.*, the cost of adding one more unit, is below price, the producer can add more to his receipts than to his costs by producing more. When marginal cost is above price, it means that some units are being produced at a loss and the producer will gain by contracting his output. Over a wide range of output, marginal costs will fall as output is increased. Beyond a certain point, an expansion of output will result in rising costs, *i.e.*, will be subject to diminishing returns, but such expansion may take place so long as the cost of the marginal output, *i.e.*, the cost of the last unit produced, is just covered by the selling price. The costs per unit of the marginal producers, and the costs of the marginal output of the more efficient producers, are both what are known as *marginal costs*, and represent the cost of producing the most expensive part of the supply provided by those producers to satisfy the current demand.

The only difference is that the more efficient firms will be producing at a lower average cost, which may be considerably below price, and they will be making greater profit, corresponding with their greater efficiency.

PRICE MUST COVER MARGINAL COST

Now, buyers of a certain commodity require a certain supply of that commodity, and the price offered must cover the marginal cost of such a supply, otherwise supply will be reduced to a lower level, and part of the demand will be unsatisfied. If demand decreases to such an extent that price falls below marginal cost, then existing marginal producers (*i.e.*, producers who are just paying their way) go out of business and a new set of marginal producers, with lower costs, take their place. In addition, the more efficient producers produce fewer units, in order to reduce their marginal costs to the new lower price.

If, on the other hand, demand increases, the greater supply now required will be forthcoming only if price rises sufficiently to make it profitable for a lower grade of producer, hitherto sub-marginal, with higher costs to enter into production, and to stimulate the more efficient producers to expand their outputs, involving higher marginal costs.

A change in price may not be *immediately* followed by a change in output. If price rises, it may not be possible to increase output appreciably; and if price falls, marginal producers may prefer to go on producing their former output rather than to shut down and realise capital assets at a loss; but in the long run, if a given supply is required, *the price offered must cover the marginal costs of all producers contributing to the supply*.

Occasionally it may happen that an expansion of output will lead to lower marginal costs because of the operation of increasing returns; but more usually producers, without waiting for an increase in demand, will have expanded output to the point where any further expansion will lead to diminishing returns and increased marginal costs. Hence, if the technique of production remains the same, an increase in output almost invariably means rising marginal costs.

If the technique of production is improved, however, as frequently happens, an increased output can be produced at a lower cost. Changes in demand exercise the most important influence on prices in the short run; but, in the long run, influences from the side of supply, due to changes in the cost of production, are generally more important than changes in demand.

THE REAL COST OF PRODUCTION

So far we have analysed the nature of the costs incurred in production, but we have not considered how these costs are measured. Usually, they are measured in terms of *money*—so much rent is paid for a factory, so much money for coal or other sources of power, so much for labour, and so on. But even where money is *not* used (as in a community where exchange is carried on by barter), or when the article produced is not sold or bartered for another article, production still involves cost. How, then, are we to measure cost of production in such a way that it will be valid for all times and in all conditions?

The real cost of producing a commodity may be defined *as the alternative commodities that could have been produced with the resources used in the production of that commodity*. The cost of the coal, labour and raw materials used in production depends on the strength of the various kinds of demand which compete for the use of those things the supplies of which are, of course, limited. All such resources are scarce and can be put to several uses; when they are used to produce one thing, they cannot be used to produce anything else, and the alternatives sacrificed measure the *real* cost of producing the original commodity.

THE COST OF DESTRUCTION

It has been said that earthquakes and war are good for trade because the restoration of the devastated areas and, in the case of war, the provision of munitions and other military equipment provide work for large numbers of people. A consideration of the *real* costs of war soon disposes of this fallacy. The cost of war is not represented by the prices paid for the guns, tanks, ammunition, ships, etc., but *by the alternative commodities that could have been produced with the resources used*. If the Nation's resources were not used to produce armaments and munitions, they might be employed in ways that would greatly increase the national welfare: for instance, in building clean and comfortable homes for those who live in slums, or in providing schools, universities, recreation grounds, hospitals and also homes for the elderly.

Destruction of any sort, even a broken window-pane, is not good for the community *as a whole*, although particular interests, such as glaziers, may benefit. By any such form of destruction capital resources are destroyed or reduced, and their replacement withdraws labour and capital from employment in channels where they could have been used to increase the existing supplies of producers' and consumers' goods. The restoration of destroyed property leaves the Nation no better off than it was before the destruction.

When a nation goes to war, both the existing generation and posterity have to bear the real cost of the war. The community is deprived not only of valuable existing materials and property, but also of the goods necessary for the welfare of a progressive community, that could have been produced with the resources used for the provision of the arms and equipment of war.

CHAPTER VI

HOW THINGS WE NEED ARE VALUED

PRODUCTION is not complete until the finished goods have reached the hands of the consumer. The process by which this is achieved is known as *marketing*, and is an important aspect of the productive organisation.

MARKETS

A "market" originally meant a *place* where goods were bought and sold. Every village had its market-place to which the farmer, tailor, carpenter and other producers brought their goods for sale to their neighbours. The term "market" to-day has a much wider, frequently a world-wide, significance. It refers, not to any particular *locality* where goods are bought and sold, but rather to a *set of conditions* which allow the buyers and sellers of a commodity to get into touch with one another, and which permit competition between buyers on the one hand and between sellers on the other. There is a market for every commodity that has buyers and sellers, even though there is no specified place where they meet.

All that is required to constitute a market, therefore, is a commodity that can be bought and sold, some people who are willing to buy, and others who are willing to sell. The buyers and sellers can communicate with one another by word of mouth, or by letter, or by telephone, cable or wireless; the method or place does not matter so long as there is sufficient contact between the people on the market to establish competition to buy or to sell. In a *perfect market*, competition is entirely free, communication is rapid and easy, and there are many buyers and sellers.

Naturally, the size of the market varies according to the nature of the commodity, and according to the number of people who wish to deal in it. Thus there are world-wide markets for certain stock-exchange securities, for many metals such as gold, silver and tin; for important raw materials and food such as wool, cotton, rubber and wheat. On the other hand, the markets for very perishable goods (such as flowers) or for cheap goods of a bulky nature (such as building materials) are narrow and restricted.

The commodities for which there is a wide market are those that are in universal demand, durable, safely transportable and easily graded, so that samples can be taken and the goods exactly described. Such commodities can be bought and sold by persons living at a great distance both from one another and from the commodities themselves. Indeed, buyers and sellers may never see or handle the goods in which they deal, as is the case with the great markets in cotton, wheat and rubber.

Commodities that are not in wide demand, that are difficult to transport and cannot be easily graded, have only narrow markets. The market for distinctive millinery, for instance, is very limited.

VALUE

Buyers and sellers meet on the market and goods exchange hands. The buyer of flowers or vegetables gives money in exchange for these articles, and the amount of money he gives depends upon the *value* of the commodities.

Value is the power a commodity has of commanding in exchange for itself other commodities or services. If eight loaves of bread can be exchanged for twenty-four bananas, the value of one loaf in terms of bananas is three. The value of any article, therefore, is the measure of the sacrifice the seller makes in parting with the article and of the sacrifice the buyer makes in order to obtain that article. Value thus *expresses a relationship between one commodity and another*, and this relationship varies from time to time, from place to place, and from person to person.

The value of a commodity at any particular time and in any particular place *depends upon how scarce the commodity is* at that time and in that place, and how much it is wanted, *i.e., value depends on supply and demand*. Generally, it may be said that if supply is small in relation to demand, value is high; whereas if supply is plentiful in relation to demand, value is low.

In tropical countries a suit of clothes exchanges for more bananas than it does in a temperate country where bananas are not plentiful.

PRICE

In developed communities, of course, goods are not exchanged directly for other goods. Goods are exchanged for *money*, and that money is exchanged for other goods. The value of goods to us and to others is expressed in terms of money, and *value in terms of money is called price*. In other words, price is the money measure of value.

Price plays an important part in most economic systems. In them, the *pricing process* determines the allocation of resources and indicates the activities in which the agents of production can be most profitably employed. Movements in the prices of goods and services indicate whether more or less of these commodities ought to be produced in the future. A heavy fall in the price of a commodity indicates that more is coming on the market than is demanded by consumers. Production should, therefore, be curtailed. A sharp rise in price means that there is not enough of a commodity on the market to satisfy the demand, and that an increase in production would be profitable. *Prices, therefore, act as a barometer to production*; they indicate how factors of production can be used to the best advantage, *i.e.*, in the most profitable manner.

THE LAW OF INDIFFERENCE

In a perfect market there *can be only one price for a given commodity at any particular time.* If two prices prevailed, all the buyers would buy from the seller whose price was the lower, and the other sellers would find themselves with unsold stocks. Such a situation is not possible in a perfect market, because it is the essence of such a market that information shall travel quickly, so that a seller who discovered that his price was too high would at once lower it. This tendency towards a single price at a given time is known as the *Law of Indifference.*

HOW IS MARKET PRICE FIXED?

How, then, is this single price arrived at in a market? Imagine a market where many buyers are present to buy a quantity of goods brought there by many sellers. Buyers compete with buyers to obtain the goods, and sellers compete with sellers to sell them. Out of this seemingly complex situation, one single price will emerge at which business will be done.

We will consider the sellers first. Each seller knows what he must get from the sale of *all* his goods if he is to make a profit, but, if no market price has already been fixed, he will be prepared to sell a certain number at various prices, the number depending on his need for cash and his reluctance to take the goods home. Suppose we are in the vegetable market. The green peas one seller has to offer have cost 6p per lb. to produce, including normal profit, and he has brought 500 lb. to the market. If he can get 6p per lb., he will be willing to sell the 500 lb. But suppose he can get only 5p per lb., what will he do?

If he sells all the 500 lb. at this price, he will certainly make too great a loss. On the other hand, if he sells none at all, he must take all his stock home again and wait for a higher price. But there is no certainty that the price will rise before the peas go bad; it may even fall below 5p.

Now our seller of peas may decide to sell none below 6p per lb.; but he will more probably decide to sell, say, 400 lb. at 5p. By so doing, he gets some ready cash, disposes of some of his stock, and retains 100 lb. to sell the next day, when the price may be higher. Actually, the seller of peas will have in his mind a scale of the number of pounds of peas he will sell at various prices, e.g., he will sell 500 at 6p, 400 at 5p and 300 at 4p. At a lower price than this he may sell none at all, thinking it better to hold his stock for a short time in the hope of a rise in price, rather than suffer a heavy loss now.

Since each seller on the market has some such scale in his mind, we can, by adding the various scales together, get an idea of how many pounds of peas the sellers as a body will be prepared to sell at various prices. Each seller has different costs and has, therefore, a different scale of how many pounds of peas he will sell at different prices; but one rule is common to all, viz., each will sell fewer pounds at a lower price, and more at a higher price. Some sellers will want to dispose of some, at least, of their peas, perhaps even at a price below the cost of production. Our combined *sellers' schedule* will, therefore, look something like this:—

2,000 lb. will be supplied at a price of 6p
1,600 ,, ,, ,, ,, 5p
1,200 lb. will be supplied at a price of 4p
800 ,, ,, ,, ,, 3p
400 ,, ,, ,, ,, 2p

The buyers also come to the market with the intention of buying a certain quantity of peas at a maximum average price, or different quantities at various prices, so long as the total price they have to pay does not exceed their maximum. We know from our study of diminishing utility that a person values each additional unit of a stock of goods less than he valued the previous unit, and that the price he is willing to pay for the marginal unit is the price he pays for all units. One buyer may be willing to buy 100 lb. of peas at 6p per lb., 150 lb. at 5p and 200 lb. at 4p. Another consumer may not be willing to buy any peas at 6p per lb., but is prepared to buy 100 lb. at 5p and 200 lb. at 4p. Just as we added together the scales of the various sellers, so we can now add together the scales of the various buyers, and then we can see what amounts buyers as a whole are prepared to buy at certain prices.

Again one rule is common to all buyers, however much their individual requirements may vary, viz., some buy more at a lower price, while others who would not buy at all at a higher price will become buyers at a lower price, and total purchases will be less at a higher price. Our combined *buyers' schedule* will be somewhat as follows:—

600 lb.	will be bought at a price of			6p
1,000	,,	,,	,,	5p
1,200 lb.	will be bought at a price of			4p
1,400	,,	,,	,,	3p
1,800	,,	,,	,,	2p
2,000	,,	,,	,,	1p

Balancing of Supply and Demand

We have now the schedules of buyers and sellers on our green pea market. If demand and supply operate freely, if there is no friction such as rationing, price fixing or credit restriction, the interaction of demand and supply will result in the emergence of the single price. We can show that under free market conditions there is only one price at which supply and demand balance.

Let us consider a price of 5p per lb. of peas. At this price, 1,600 lb. would be supplied, but only 1,000 would be bought. There is the danger, therefore, that some of the sellers who would be willing to sell at 5p might be shut out of the market altogether, since there is a surplus of 600 lb. of peas at that price. The owners of the 1,600 lb. must, therefore, accept less than 5p if they wish to reduce the risk of being left with surplus peas on their hands, owing to supply being in excess of demand. They, consequently, lower their prices. Although sellers are not willing to sell as many peas at this lower price, they know that there is now a better chance of getting a share of the market.

Now let us consider a price of 3p, at which there are sellers for 800 lb., but buyers for 1,400 lb. Some of these buyers will be willing to pay more than 3p per lb., and rather than lose their chance of getting some of the 800 lb. on offer they will raise their bids.

Let us now consider a price of 4p per lb. At this price 1,200 lb. are offered and 1,200 lb. are demanded. At a lower price, competition between buyers will cause the price to move to 4p, and at a higher price, competition between sellers will cause the price to move to 4p. But at 4p there is no force tending to make the price other than 4p.

The single price for peas on the market under the conditions we have stipulated is, therefore, 4p per lb.: at this price 1,200 lb. will be sold and 1,200 lb. will be bought. The various owners of the remaining 800 lb. offered for sale will hold back their stocks, hoping to sell them another day, whilst the people who were willing to buy another 800 lb. will postpone satisfaction of their wants until the price falls.

We can now see the truth of the statement that *"price depends on supply and demand"*. We can also see that the price at which goods change hands in a market at a particular time may be much less than the cost of production, because sellers may not want or be able to keep their goods, and have to accept what they can get for at least a part of their stock. What they can get depends on the marginal utility of their goods to buyers. On the other hand, market price may be above cost of production, and buyers may have to pay for part of their requirements more than they would be willing to pay for all they could do with at any particular time.

MARKET PRICE VARIES FROM TIME TO TIME

We see, therefore, that the market price for a commodity is the price ruling on the market at the point where the demand balances supply. The whole of the supply offered *at that price* will be taken off the market.

In the above example, 4p measures the marginal utility to each buyer of the number of lb. of peas bought, *i.e.*, the utility of the last lb. bought by each buyer. Since the marginal utility is equal for all buyers, it is clear that 4p measures the marginal utility of 1,200 lb. Market price, therefore, corresponds to the marginal utility of the quantity sold; it measures the utility to each buyer of the last unit worth buying. In other words, market price corresponds to the value of the least urgently required part of the stock sold.

The application of the principle "market price is fixed where demand and supply balance" helps us to predict what the price will be when the intentions of the sellers are different from those stipulated in the example above. Suppose the sellers as a whole bring 2,000 lb. of peas to the market and that they are prepared to get rid of them however low the price is. We can deduce from our tables that those 2,000 lb. will, in fact, be sold at the price of 1p, for at that price 2,000 lb. are demanded. Competition between sellers will force any higher price down to this level. If, on the other hand, sellers ask more than 1p per lb., competition between the buyers of 2,000 lb. at that price will drive the price above 1p.

Again, the sellers of 2,000 lb. may fix a minimum price at which they will sell, being ready to sell all they have at this price, but also prepared to take all their peas home if the price falls below that level. Suppose they fix 3p per lb. as this minimum price. Then we can predict that the market price will be 3p, that 1,400 lb. will be sold at that price and that 600 lb. will be taken home, because the demand at 3p (the *"reserve price"* of the sellers) is 1,400 lb. In fact, the sellers are the "buyers" of the remaining 600 lb. at their reserve price. Instances of sellers buying back at their reserve prices are frequently met with in auction rooms.

Market price may vary from day to day, and even at different times of the day, with changes in supply and demand. One day there may be a dearth of buyers. In a local agricultural market business is bad on wet days, and market-people at the end of the day sell their perishable goods at very low prices rather than cart them home again. On another day there may be a poor supply of, *e.g.*, apples owing to an early frost, and the price of apples will tend to be high.

DETERMINATION OF MARKET PRICE

Position at given price.	Effect on price.	Cause.
Supply exceeds demand	Price falls	Sellers compete to sell
Demand exceeds supply	Price rises	Buyers compete to buy
Demand equals supply	No effect	Price is equilibrium price

The market price of very perishable goods (*e.g.*, fresh flowers in a local market) tends to vary considerably and may be very low owing to the eagerness of the sellers to dispose of their stocks. If the goods are durable, sellers are more inclined to hold back their stocks when the price is low, in the hope that they can sell later at higher prices. But even with *non-perishable* goods there are marked variations in price. Clothes for which the appeal is mainly seasonal are disposed of at low prices at the end-of-season sales.

Market price is a *short-period* price. It is a price determined in conditions that do not allow for adjustments in supply.

NORMAL PRICE

We showed in the previous chapter that producers as a whole tend to adjust their output so that the price at which they sell covers the marginal costs of production. If price rises above marginal costs, the industry will show large profits, some producers will expand their output and new producers will enter the industry until the increased supplies bring about a fall in price. Conversely, if price falls below marginal costs, some producers contract their outputs, other producers leave the industry, and price rises.

But the price that producers thus take into consideration obviously cannot be the market price that rules on any particular day, because that price, as we have seen, varies considerably according to the conditions of demand and supply on the market concerned at the particular time, and may bear no relation to cost of production.

The price that producers have to consider before they decide to increase or to decrease their output must obviously be a *long-period price*; and in respect of every commodity there is, in fact, a sort of middle price or equilibrium price about which market price fluctuates, now above and now below, during the long period.

Market Price and Normal Price of an Article

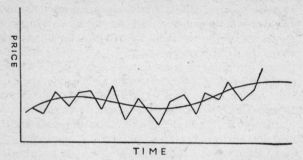

The smooth curve represents normal price, which itself may change owing to developments in technique or owing to changes in the prices of raw materials, etc.

The other curve represents the frequent fluctuations of market price above and below normal price.

The housewife who does her weekly shopping every Saturday morning knows that the prices she pays vary from time to time. She never knows exactly what she will have to pay when she is making out her shopping list, but she knows approximately what the prices are likely to be at a certain time of the year. A particular commodity may be 4p per lb. this week and 6p per lb. next week, but before she enters the shop the housewife knows that the price she will have to pay will be about 5p, *i.e.*, she knows that the normal price for this particular commodity is 5p per lb. Similarly, a normal price applies in the case of all other commodities that are bought and sold.

The long-period price about which market price fluctuates is called *normal price*, and, in the case of goods that are readily reproducible, *normal price tends to equal marginal cost of production*. For a time, market price might be higher than normal price, but the high price (and so the extra profit that can be obtained) will attract other producers; supply will increase and price will fall. If market price falls and remains below normal price, *i.e.*, below marginal cost of production, marginal producers will leave the industry and take their resources where they can be more profitably employed, other producers will contract their outputs, supply will fall and prices will rise.

In certain cases, market price and normal price tend to coincide. There is little or no difference between the market price and normal price of things in regular, general demand, such as scrubbing-brushes or toothpaste, because their supply can be easily adjusted to market conditions.

In fact, the easier it is to adjust supply to demand, the closer the relation at any time between market price and cost of production. In the case of goods whose supply is fixed for all time, *e.g.*, old masters and antiques, there is no cost of production that can be considered, and price, therefore, has no relation to cost. The price of a painting by Rembrandt or of an early edition of Shakespeare's plays depends solely on demand. The price has no relation to the work put into such things by the painter or author; it depends entirely on what certain collectors are willing to pay.

Again, the short-period or market price of very perishable goods, such as strawberries, bears little relation to cost of production. Producers take what they can get. Because of the time it takes to grow strawberries, the supply cannot quickly be increased to meet a very strong demand, and, because of the perishability of the fruit, the supply cannot profitably be decreased when the demand is small by taking some of the fruit off the market. But when a long period is considered, producers of strawberries must get a sufficient return to keep them in the business. The high price they get during the "out-of-season" period must make up for the low price they get when strawberries are in season and the supply on the market is more than enough to satisfy the demand. If the normal price did not cover marginal costs, some producers would give up strawberry-growing and the normal price of strawberries would rise until it bore a closer relation to their cost of production both in and out of season.

CHAPTER VII

MONOPOLIES AND MONOPOLY PRICE

So far in our consideration of the economic aspect of life we have assumed conditions of *free competition*. We have not allowed for any interference with buyers competing among themselves, or with sellers competing with one another. Actually, however, free competition is not always the case. The housewife who finds prices higher in one shop than in another can change her retailer; but, if she feels that the price of coal from one dealer is too high, she cannot do better by changing her tradesman in order to get a lower price, because the coal industry has been nationalised and the National Coal Board has a monopoly of coal in Britain. The Board therefore fixes the price at which coal is bought and sold.

We find the same position in regard to certain other things. We cannot buy electricity or gas or water from one of several suppliers and choose to deal with the one that charges the lowest price. We have to obtain each of these things from the local suppliers and pay them the price they ask. In the same way, we cannot choose who shall carry our letters or how much we shall pay for stamps; we cannot choose between different suppliers of telephone and telegram facilities, and we cannot argue about the price we have to pay for such conveniences. The concerns that supply us with these goods and services have a monopoly, *i.e.*, they have *the sole right to deal in these goods and services*. We have to pay the price they ask, and that price is not fixed in the same way as prices that are subject to conditions of free competition.

Apart from State-owned industries, *absolute* monopoly

is rare. Although Imperial Chemical Industries are able to control the price of some detergents and soaps because they produce such a large part of the supply, their monopoly is not absolute. Other firms produce soaps, etc., but I.C.I. are in a position to dominate the market because they make such an important contribution to the amount supplied. *Hence any firm that produces such a high proportion of the total output of a commodity that it can influence price by regulating supply is said to have a monopoly of that commodity.*

KINDS OF MONOPOLY

There are various kinds of monopoly.

NATURAL MONOPOLIES are those that arise because of limited supplies of raw material. An example of a natural monopoly is the nickel supply of Canada (about 90 per cent. of the world supply). The limited supply has created a monopoly sufficiently strong to influence the world price of the product although there are metals that can be substituted.

SOCIAL MONOPOLIES are those concerned with the supply of water, gas and electricity; and with the control of postal and telephone facilities. The concerns that supply these services have a monopoly that is necessitated by the *technical conditions of supply*; it is impracticable or even impossible for more than one concern to engage in these industries in a given area without great public inconvenience and a great waste of resources. Imagine the difficulty of telephoning your doctor if there were several telephone companies and you patronised one and he another. Consider how inconvenient it would be if half a dozen gas or electric-light undertakings had the right to dig up our roads and pavements.

In another group are the so-called LEGAL MONOPOLIES, *i.e.*, monopolies conferred and protected by law, with a view to preventing unfair competition and to giving producers, authors and inventors an opportunity to reap the reward of their efforts. Patents and copyrights are legal monopolies that confer the sole rights on certain persons to sell certain commodities and to use certain articles.

There are other classes of monopoly for which there is less justification as, for example, the monopoly acquired by firms of producers who have combined with one another in order to eliminate free competition. Their object is to safeguard the profits of the individual producers belonging to the combine by controlling or fixing the price at which the product is sold, or by controlling the output of the product so that the supply offered on the market will not be so great as to cause prices to fall below a certain level. Monopolies of this kind and restrictive practices that operate against the public interest are illegal in Britain and also in other countries (see page 82).

State-owned industries in Britain are organised as monopolies, controlled by public corporations or boards and operated in most cases by regional boards.

MONOPOLIES OF SERVICES

Although most monopolies are concerned with the supply of commodities, some of the most powerful monopolies are those that control the supply of services, as, for example, the monopolistic control of doctors' services in Britain by the General Medical Council. This Council, in the exercise of powers conferred upon it by law, restricts the practice of medicine and surgery to registered practitioners who have passed certain tests of technical knowledge and have satisfied certain prescribed conditions, and to this extent the supply of doctors in Britain may be said to be in the hands of a monopoly—fortunately, one that recognises the traditions of the profession and its obligations to the community.

In the same way a strong *trade union* may be regarded as a monopoly of a certain class of labour. In so far as trade unions limit the number of entrants to the trade and oppose the use by employers of non-union labour, and in so far also as they insist on standard rates of wages, they exercise a limited monopoly power and thus exert an effect on the price of labour similar to that of a manufacturing combination on the price of its products.

MONOPOLY PRICE

The fact that a firm possesses a monopoly does not necessarily imply that the firm can extract as high a price as possible for its commodity or service. Actually, most of the great industrial combinations that have reached a monopolistic position aim at increased profits, not by raising price against the consumer, but by lowering their costs of production by (1) large-scale organisation and concentration of production at the best-equipped plants, which are worked at full capacity; (2) eliminating wasteful competition in advertising and salesmanship; and (3) standardising the product or service, and thus increasing the general productivity of their organisation.

Moreover, every monopolist has to remember that the charging of a very high price would in most cases encourage the entry of new producers or stimulate the invention and consumption of substitutes, as well as lead to State interference with the monopoly in order to protect consumers.

It follows, therefore, that the control of prices even in the case of a very powerful monopoly is considerably limited. A monopolist may, of course, charge whatever price he pleases, but as a general rule too high a price will ultimately work to his disadvantage. The question therefore arises: At what price is the monopolist to sell in order to obtain the greatest net revenue, under all the conditions (including those of demand) which he knows to exist?

The monopolist, like any other business man, wants to obtain the highest possible profit; he tries to sell his product at a price likely to yield him the greatest surplus of total receipts over total costs. He can adopt one of two ways: he can sell as much of his product as he likes at a low and attractive price, *or* he can charge what price he likes for a small supply. *But he cannot do both*—he cannot sell as much as he likes at any price he likes. His price, if he does not fix it himself, must be determined, like that of any producer subject to free competition, by demand and supply. Demand is something beyond the monopolist's control; his attention must, therefore, be directed to supply or to price. He will, in most cases, sell more of his goods at a lower price than at a higher price. Whether or not he will charge a high price depends on the degree of elasticity of demand for the product and on the conditions of its production, *i.e.*, whether his industry is subject to increasing or decreasing returns.

If the monopolist, producing under increasing returns, charges a high price, the demand for his product will be small, his output will be small and his cost per unit will probably be higher than if his output were larger. If he now reduces his price, his sales may so increase that the gain on the extra turnover (obtained under increasing returns at less cost per unit) more than compensates for the smaller profit per article.

It will be clear, therefore, that selling at the highest price or selling the greatest possible number of articles does not necessarily mean the largest profit for the monopolist.

If the demand for the monopolist's product is *elastic* and increasing returns operate, monopoly price is likely to be low, because the cost per unit of producing a large supply is smaller than the cost per unit of a small supply. A large demand at a low price ensures the greatest net revenue.

If the demand for the monopolist's product is *inelastic*, and there are no readily available substitutes, the monopolist can charge a high price, and he can do so whatever the conditions of production. But if substitutes are available, the monopolist cannot fix the price of his own product very greatly to his advantage unless he can get control of the substitutes. For, if he charges a high price for his own product and does not control the price of the substitutes, demand will be transferred from his product to the substitutes.

Even when there are no substitutes, a monopolist who charges a very high price for a commodity for which the demand is inelastic may not be able to maintain that price without running the risk of Government interference. The Government may regulate the price that can be charged in order to avoid exploitation of the public.

It follows, therefore, that *monopoly price is not inevitably a high price*. Even from the monopolist's own point of view, the price need not be high, because, by keeping the price low and so inducing a large demand, he can increase the efficiency of his productive machinery and so keep his costs to a very low level. He can reap the economies of producing on a large scale and of the concentration of production at the best-equipped plants, of eliminating part of the costs of advertising and salesmanship, and of standardising the product. In general, large demand at a low price helps him to increase the general productivity of his organisation. In short, he can take full advantage of the economies of scale.

We can illustrate this by reference to the case of the well-known motor-car manufacturer, the late Henry

Ford, who at one time had such a monopoly of the manufacture of light cars that the old-type "Ford car" was known practically all over the world. Mr. Ford's monopoly power was restricted, however, by the possible competition of substitutes (*i.e.*, other light and cheap cars), and so his power to raise prices was definitely limited. At the same time, the sales of Ford cars would have been large even if the price had been raised, say, by one-third. The cars, however, sold at a very low price for two reasons: (1) they were produced under conditions of increasing returns; (2) the demand for cars of this type is highly elastic: normally a fall in price immediately leads to an increase in demand. Thus, in practice, Mr. Ford found it most profitable (apart from any moral considerations that might have influenced him) not to exercise the monopoly power he possessed and charge a high price for his car.

Monopoly Price and Costs

Under free competition, the individual producer produces up to the point where his marginal cost equals the price of his product. Until that point is reached, there is always a gain to be had from producing more. The individual producer does not gain by limiting his output in the hope that by so doing price will rise; all that would happen then is that other producers would produce more than before. The price would remain what it was, and the other producers would make larger profits, provided their marginal costs did not exceed price.

The monopolist is in a different position. He can very often gain by limiting his output, because there are no competitors to produce more and so bring down price. The monopolist, therefore, does not tend to equate marginal cost and price. As he is responsible for the whole output, a variation in his own output *will* affect price.

When he chooses to sell more, he has to remember that he will get less not only for the additional units, but also for the same number of units as he previously sold.

Suppose he produces motor-cars. He may be selling ten per day at £500 each. If he wants to sell eleven, he may find that he can sell them only at £480 each. The addition to his receipts will then not be £480, but £480 *minus* ten times £20, as, in the same market, he has to sell each of the first ten cars at £20 less. The addition to his receipts is thus only £280, although each car is sold for £480. He will, therefore, increase his output only if the eleventh car can be produced at less than £280. In general, a monopolist will increase output only to the point where *marginal cost equals the addition to his total receipts*; and not to the point where marginal cost equals price.

PRICE DISCRIMINATION

The monopolist has a special privilege that is not available to the competing producer. He need not sell all his output at a uniform price; he can, owing to the absence of competition, discriminate in respect of different markets and charge a different price in each. We know that surgeons frequently discriminate between patients in the fees they charge for their services. The surgeon often charges more for operating on one patient than on another; he may charge one private patient £100 for an operation for which he may charge another person only £50. A railway also discriminates as between the goods it carries, charging more for furniture than for coal. Publishers frequently issue the same book in several editions, some very expensive, some quite cheap. Again, a manufacturer may sell goods abroad at a much lower price than he charges at home for the same product.

The usual aim of discrimination is to increase profit. By judiciously fixing different prices to suit various markets, monopolistic producers can sell more goods and make a larger profit than if they fixed a uniform price for all their goods. This is particularly so where they can benefit from the economies of scale, because their costs per unit fall as their output increases.

But a monopolist can discriminate in this way only where the commodity sold in the cheaper market cannot or will not be transferred and resold to the dearer market. A poor patient cannot re-sell his doctor's services at a higher price. The industrial user of electricity at low rates cannot re-sell his electricity at higher rates to domestic users. The success of a discriminating monopolist depends, therefore, on a very efficient knowledge of the market for his goods and of the psychology of the people who purchase them.

DUMPING

Dumping usually implies the selling of goods in a foreign market at a lower price than is charged in the home market, or at a price that is below the cost of production of similar goods in the country to which they are sold. Dumping is a device frequently resorted to by monopolistic undertakings, and may be adopted in order to capture foreign markets, or to dispose of a surplus of goods produced as a result of an incorrect estimation of demand, or in order to increase output so as to obtain the economies of scale.

For instance, a manufacturer who wishes to obtain the benefits of production on a large scale may be prepared to dispose of that portion of his produce not required for his home market *at any price* so long as the price covers his prime cost of production per unit of the product. Naturally, the difference between the home and foreign price must be less than the cost of return freight *plus* the amount of any tariff which may be imposed on the goods, otherwise the goods would be bought in the foreign market and re-exported to the home market.

Dumping in order to capture foreign markets was in the past practised on a considerable scale, particularly by Germany in the then unprotected markets of Britain and of other countries. As a rule, those who resort to this method of dumping maintain low prices for the dumped products in the foreign market until the local producers are driven out of competition, and then, having achieved total or partial monopoly, they raise prices in order to increase their profits.

Such methods are necessarily disadvantageous to the purchasing country: they result in fluctuations in prices, in dislocation of trade, and may cause loss and hardship to producers of goods similar to those dumped. Nowadays, Governments prevent the dumping of foreign goods in their markets by refusing them entry, by limiting them to a quota, or by subjecting them to heavy tariffs.

CONTROL OF MONOPOLIES AND RESTRICTIVE PRACTICES

The *Monopolies and Restrictive Practices Act* of 1948 set up the *Monopolies Commission* to investigate concerns exercising monopoly and restrictive practices (*i.e.*, where entry of goods or services is restricted in some way and thus there is an element of monopoly given to those in that occupation or service) and to refer to Parliament those that are found to be against the public interest. By the *Monopolies and Mergers Act* 1965 proposed mergers may be referred by the Department of Trade to the Commission and reported to Parliament, which takes any necessary action.

Restrictive practices are covered by the *Restrictive Trade Practices Act* 1956, which set up the *Restrictive Practices Court* to which practices in dispute are referred. The Court also deals with resale price maintenance.

CHAPTER VIII

MONEY, PRICES AND BANKING

IN the economic system all values are measured in terms of *money*. We sell our services and our goods for money, and exchange that money for other goods and services that we require.

MONEY

If you ask a boy what he regards as money, he will probably pull out of his pocket a 1p or a 5p piece and tell you that is money. Of course, he will add, there are also £5 and £1 notes and 10p and 50p pieces, but he is not likely to mention gold sovereigns or half-sovereigns. He belongs to a generation that has never seen gold in circulation.

WHAT IS MONEY?

For small transactions in this country we use coins of cupro-nickel and bronze. These coins are known as *token money*, because the value of the metal contained in each is less than the face value of the coin. If a 5p piece were melted down the resulting mixture would be worth less than the face value of the coin. For the majority of our transactions we use *paper money*, *i.e.*, Bank of England notes of £1, £5, £10 and £20.

Each of these forms of money is a *medium of exchange*, *i.e.*, something that we can give in exchange for some article or service that we require. We sell our services for money in the form of wages or salaries, and use that money to buy things we want—food, clothing, shelter, cigarettes and seats at the cinema.

Money, therefore, is a means whereby we exchange our goods and services for the goods and services that we need to satisfy our wants. And the money we pay to the shopkeeper or cinema proprietor enables him, in turn, to exchange the goods or services he sells for other things that he needs. *Money is, in fact, anything that is widely used and accepted within a community as a means of exchange.*

VARIOUS KINDS OF MONEY

Before money took the form of coins and bank notes, many other things were used as media of exchange. As a rule, such things were commodities in fairly general use or ownership. Cattle served that purpose in early pastoral communities, while slaves, furs, skins, shells, tea, tobacco and rice have been used at various times and in various places. But to us the use of any such things would appear to be highly inconvenient, and we should certainly not regard them as fulfilling the functions of a *good money*. Slaves and cattle cannot be sub-divided and have only a limited life; tea, tobacco and rice perish. They cannot be held indefinitely as a *store of value*. This is a great inconvenience, because people who sell things for money are not always in immediate need of the things they could get in exchange; they want something they can keep until they need to use it. Consequently, they must have as money something that can be put on one side for use at a later date without loss of value. From early times the precious metals, gold and silver, were found to be admirable for this purpose and gradually they came into general use, first as unshaped pieces of varying weights, but later in the form of *coins* of standard weight issued under the authority of the State and stamped with an easily recognisable device to testify to their genuineness.

Although most countries, at some periods in the past, have preferred silver to gold, gold by the end of the nineteenth century was established as the money standard for practically the whole world. But gold is very expensive and, in addition, the supplies of the metal have become inadequate to meet the ever-increasing needs of exchange, particularly of international exchange. Hence bank notes have been substituted for gold for internal use and the gold thus released was made available for monetary reserves and for making foreign payments.

THE MONEY-WORK

What is the work that money is required to do? Broadly, money has to do two things: it must act as a *medium of exchange* or intermediary between goods and

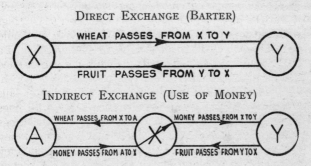

goods, and it must serve as a *unit of account, i.e.,* a unit in terms of which business transactions can be measured and recorded. Without a medium of exchange we should have to exchange one article directly for another article: so much butter for a pound of tea; so much milk for a loaf of bread. Every time a hatter wanted a shave, he would have to find a barber who wanted a hat. In other words, we should have to resort to *barter*, the direct exchange of goods and services for other goods and services, without the intervention of money. Obviously, this system is extremely inconvenient and not always possible. In a modern community there must be a medium of exchange, which people will freely accept for their goods and services and can keep until such time as they wish to use it for the purchase of other goods and services.

It is also important that there should be a *unit of account*, to provide us with a standard by means of which we can measure and record the values of things exchanged. When we use money we express each thing entering into exchange as worth so many units of money, *i.e.*, everything of value has a *price*, and by using money we can without difficulty compare the relative values of any two things. If a loaf of bread and a pint of milk each costs, say, about 5p, we know that a 5p loaf has the same value, as a pint of milk. If a hat costs £1·50 and a shave 10p, we know at once that the hat is worth 15 shaves, and so on.

Anything used as money must perform these two functions. At one time, money was also expected to serve as a *store of value*, *i.e.*, to be put away until it was wanted without losing any of its value as a means of exchange for other goods. Obviously, money has ceased to be stable in value and anyone who wants to hold a store of value now prefers to hold works of art, precious metals or jewels, or landed property.

Akin to this is the function of acting as a *standard for deferred payments*. The value of money was, indeed, stable over a long period, but it is no longer so. The value of most currencies continues to fall and people have become chary of making long-term contracts in such currencies.

GOLD AS MONEY

Gold was, in the past, a satisfactory form of money. It is universally *acceptable* because it has alternative uses for adornment, in the arts, in dentistry, and so on. Gold is also easily recognised, portable and durable, whilst it can be divided into small pieces or coins of uniform quality without losing any of its value. Further, it has great value in small bulk, and over long periods its value was comparatively steady; it was, therefore, an acceptable store of value.

Other metals also have certain of these qualities, though to a less degree than gold. Silver, for example, is far more plentiful, and consequently far less expensive than gold, but its value has been subject to more marked fluctuations. Hence in practically all countries silver was gradually superseded by gold as the standard of value but gold is no longer stable in value and as we saw above is no longer a store of value.

PAPER MONEY

As gold coins are expensive to use and as there is not nearly enough gold in the world to settle all transactions, modern communities use as money paper notes of various denominations. Paper money generally comprises *bank notes*, *i.e.*, notes issued by an authorised bank (*e.g.*, the £1, £5, £10 and £20 notes of the Bank of England), and less frequently *government notes*, *i.e.*, notes issued by the State.

Notes are *convertible* when the holder has a legal right to return them to the issuer for exchange into gold or silver, whichever is the standard metal. Notes are *inconvertible* when no such right exists. For many years before the Great War of 1914–1918, the Bank of England note was fully convertible into gold coin or bullion, and it remained convertible until the Gold Standard was suspended in 1931. The Bank of England now does not give gold in exchange for its notes. It keeps securities and a small amount of coins as a backing for its note issues. Like Britain most industrialised countries have bank notes that are inconvertible but backed by reserves of securities and gold held by the Government or the central bank. To-day, gold currency reserves are negligible, practically the whole note issues being fiduciary, as they are in Britain.

LEGAL TENDER MONEY

Usually, the money that you carry in your pocket for buying things—money such as Bank of England notes, and coins—will be what is called *legal tender*. The law decrees that certain forms of money *must* be accepted by the person to whom you offer it in exchange for goods or services, or in payment of an outstanding account. In other words, it can be legally offered, or *tendered*, to your creditor, and your creditor cannot legally refuse to accept it, although he could refuse to accept money that was not legal tender, *e.g.*, the notes or the money of another country, or a cheque.

Money that is legal tender is the *currency* of the country. The law may declare that a given form of money is legal tender for payment of *any amount* (*i.e.*, *unlimited* legal tender), or legal tender for payments *only up to a certain amount* (*i.e.*, *limited* legal tender). In Britain, Bank of England notes are unlimited tender; you can use them to pay a debt of any amount and your creditor prejudices his rights to payment if he refuses to accept them. Cupro-nickel coins and bronze coins, however, are limited legal tender. Therefore, if you owed a person £5 and offered to pay him 500 pence, he would have the right to refuse your offer and could sue you for proper payment. Such money is *token money*: its real value is less than its face value.

BANK MONEY

In practice, currency or *cash* (which is another name for currency) is used to settle transactions of only quite moderate amount. As a rule, currency is not used for settling large business transactions. The majority of business payments are made by using bank money consisting of bank notes (which are legal tender in England and Wales and subject to legal control) and bank deposits. *Bank deposits* constitute the largest part of the supply of money to-day; they are operated by means of *cheques* which, briefly, are orders to a bank to transfer a stated amount of money from the account of one person to another person, *i.e.*, to transfer a part of the bank deposit of one person to the bank deposit of another person. This form of money is not legal tender but it is accepted by creditors in payment for goods or in settlement of debts, provided the drawer is considered to be reliable.

CREDIT INSTRUMENTS

These exist in various forms (bills of exchange, promissory notes, postal orders and money orders) and are used to settle an enormous number of transactions, thereby economising legal tender. They are *substitutes* for legal tender, and are accepted because the person receiving them counts on being able to convert them into cash without difficulty, if he wishes to do so.

FORMS OF MONEY

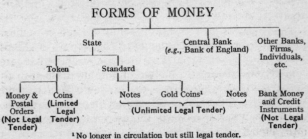

	State		Central Bank *(e.g.*, Bank of England)		Other Banks, Firms, Individuals, etc.
Token		Standard			
Money & Postal Orders (Not Legal Tender)	Coins (Limited Legal Tender)	Notes	Gold Coins[1]	Notes	Bank Money and Credit Instruments (Not Legal Tender)
			(Unlimited Legal Tender)		

[1] No longer in circulation but still legal tender.

The Value of Money

We have seen that the value of any commodity, *i.e.*, its power of exchanging for other commodities, is determined by the interaction of demand and supply. Money is no different from any other commodity: its value, *i.e.*, its power of exchanging for goods, or its *purchasing power* over commodities, also depends on demand and supply.

The Demand for Money is the quantity of money needed to effect business transactions; *i.e.*, to effect the transfer or exchange of the goods and services offered for sale. Sellers want money for their goods and services; in other words, they are demanding money, and the more goods and services there are being exchanged, the greater is the demand for money.

The same article, as it passes from producer to wholesaler, wholesaler to retailer and retailer to consumer, may give rise to a demand for money from several people. The demand for money is, therefore, affected not only by the volume of goods and services being exchanged, but also by the *frequency* with which such goods are exchanged, as is indicated by the number of people through whose hands the goods pass before reaching the final consumer. The greater the *activity* of trade, *i.e.*, the *velocity of circulation of goods*, as distinct from the volume of trade, the greater the demand for money.

The Supply of Money is the actual amount of money —notes, coins, bank deposits, bills, etc.—used for effecting exchanges. It includes all forms of money that are doing the money-work. But in considering the supply of money, we must consider not merely the total quantity of money in use, but also the *velocity of circulation of money*, *i.e.*, the number of separate transactions for which each unit of money is used. The five pence we give the baker is passed by him to his wife, who in turn hands it over to the greengrocer in payment for a cabbage or potatoes. The same coin used in ten transactions is really performing the same function as ten separate coins each used in one transaction only. The velocity of circulation thus increases the supply of money engaged in doing the money work.

Now, at any moment there is a certain quantity of money being used to pay for a certain quantity of goods and services, and *it is the relation between the total supply of goods and the total supply of money that determines the value of money*. If the quantity of goods increases whilst the amount of money remains the same, each unit of money will rise or prices will fall. Every unit of money now buys more goods than it did before; an article that previously cost, say, 50p can now be purchased for only 40p. If, on the other hand, the quantity of goods remains the same and more money is made available (*e.g.*, by the issue of extra notes), the value of a unit of money falls, *i.e.*, prices rise. Whereas previously we might have been able to buy 4 lb. of a commodity for 30p, we must now pay 40p; every unit buys less of the commodity and, of course, less of everything else.

Thus the *value of money and prices in general are two aspects of the same thing*. Variations in either the demand for money or the supply of money cause variations both in the value of money and in prices, but they vary in opposite directions. Let us suppose that, on a given date, A,—

A.   2,000 units of goods equal 20,000 units of money.
     Then 1 unit of goods equals 10 units of money.

Now, suppose that, following an improvement in productive methods, the supply of goods by another date, B, is doubled, but that there is no change in the amount of money available for settling exchanges; then, on date B—

> B.   4,000 units of goods equal 20,000 units of money.
> And 1 unit of goods equals 5 units of money.

As between dates A and B, therefore, the value of the money has risen, because, at B, we can buy the same quantity of goods for less money, 5 units instead of 10.

Looking at this change from another point of view, we see that prices have fallen. Whereas at date A 10 units of money are necessary to buy 1 unit of goods, at date B only 5 units are necessary to buy the same quantity of goods. We can see, therefore, that the *value of money varies inversely as the general level of prices*. If prices rise, the value of money falls; if prices fall, the value of money rises. Further, we can see that if the supply of money remains the same whilst the demand for money increases, there is a rise in the value of money.

PRICES

Price Index Numbers

As money is itself the measuring-rod by which we indicate and determine the value of all other things, we cannot express the value of money except in terms of commodities in general; that is, *we can measure changes in the value of money only by changes in the* general *level of prices*. These changes are difficult to measure, first, because money is used in a host of different ways apart from the purchase of goods; secondly, because the prices of some goods rise whilst the prices of others fall during the same period; and, thirdly, because goods change so much in quality and description over a period of years that we cannot be certain, when we are comparing the price of one unit at one time with its price at another time, whether we are dealing with exactly the same article.

What we call the *method of index numbers* does, however, enable us to measure approximate changes in the value of money from year to year. The computation of an index number is a complicated business, but the principle can be explained by a simple example. Suppose that in 1970 we pay 9p for a loaf of bread, 36p for a pound of butter and 75p for a pound of meat. Suppose, too, that in 1971 the price of bread has fallen to 7p, that the price of butter is unchanged, but that the price of meat has risen to 50p. If now we take 1970 as the year with which we propose to compare future prices (*i.e.*, as our *base* year), we equate the prices for that year to 100, and calculate the prices in subsequent years as percentages of the prices for 1970; thus:

			1970.	1971.		
Bread	.	.	9p = 100	$7p = 7 \times \dfrac{100}{9} =$		77
Butter	.	.	36p = 100	36p =		100
Meat	.	.	75p = 100	$100p = 100 \times \dfrac{100}{75} =$		133
			3)300			3)310

Average, *i.e.*, Index Number (1970) = 100
Average, *i.e.*, Index Number (1971) = 103

Thus for 1971 we have 103 as the index number comparable with that of 100 for 1970, and this means that there was a rise of 3 per cent. in the general level of prices in 1971 as compared with 1970. In the same way we can calculate the index number for future years (and of course, for past years, if we can obtain the prices), and so we obtain figures that quickly give us an indication of the percentage rise or fall in prices as compared with the base year (1970).

In practice, the prices of a large number of different commodities and of different grades or varieties of the same commodity are taken so as to ensure greater accuracy. Moreover, *wholesale* prices of *food commodities* (*e.g.*,

wheat and beef) and *raw materials* (*e.g.*, wool and cotton)
are selected for index numbers of *general prices* because
they are more easily and accurately determined than retail prices, and because food commodities and raw
materials change little in description from one year to
another. Retail prices are, however, used as the basis of
index numbers designed to indicate and record changes
in the *cost of living*, because the commodities on which
the earnings of workers are spent are purchased at retail
prices.

WEIGHTING

In the example of an index number given above, it was
assumed for simplicity that the commodities, bread,
butter and meat, are of equal importance in the general
scheme of consumption in the community. Actually,
however, commodities are far from being of equal importance, so that an index number that is to be of any
value must make some allowance for the relative importance of the different commodities on which we spend
our money. If one commodity occupies a position of little
importance in our general expenditure, a rise in its price
should not influence disproportionately an index number
that purports to indicate changes in the *general* level of
prices; in other words, a rise in the price of that commodity should not be given too much "weight" in our
index. On the other hand, commodities that are of importance must be allowed for according to their promi-
nence in the expenditure of the average person.

For this reason, the compilers of index numbers attempt
to allow for the different importance of the commodities
whose price-changes they are measuring by assigning to
them "weights" that correspond to their relative significance in the average family "budget" or average distribution of expenditure.

Let us suppose, for example, that bread is five times

and butter twice as important as meat in the budgets of consumers as a whole. We then assign a "weight" of 5 to bread, 2 to butter and 1 to meat. Then, to obtain more accurate index numbers, we multiply the approximate weight by the ascertained new price of each commodity, expressed as a percentage of the base price, and we then divide the sum of the resulting products by the sum of the weights, thus:

	Price in 1970.	Price in 1971.	1971 1970 %.	Weights.	Product of Percentage and Weight.
Bread . .	9p	7p	77	5	385
Butter .	36p	36p	100	2	200
Meat . .	75p	100p	133	1	133
				8	8)718
					90

Weighted Index Number = 90.

The reader will see that while in this example of weighting we bring in the price of meat *once*, we bring in the price of bread *five times* and the price of butter *twice*.

CHANGES IN THE PRICE LEVEL

Individual prices are, of course, constantly changing, some rising and others falling. But, as a rule, these changes offset one another and have little serious effect. Changes in the *general level of prices* as indicated by an index number are, however, much more important and far more serious in their results.

RISING PRICES are said to be good for trade. They encourage business men to expand their businesses because rising commodity prices usually mean wider profit margins, for the reason that the manufacturer's fixed charges (such as rent, rates and interest on debentures) do not rise at all, or rise less than the prices of the goods he sells. Rising prices, therefore, usually mean that industrial plant is more fully employed, and that there is a reduction in overhead costs per unit of output.

There is also an increase in employment, *directly* because the expanding businesses require additional labour, and *indirectly* because people generally have more to spend and more goods and services have to be produced for sale. In this way prosperity is diffused throughout the community. The producing classes are, on the whole, the debtors of the community, and, as a rise in prices reduces the *real* burden of their debts and interest payments (because each unit of money they have to pay away represents less goods than before), they can more easily and successfully carry on their activities.

Rising prices are advantageous to an *industrial* nation if the rise is not violent. But when prices rise markedly, as in a period of *inflation*, considerable harm is caused, because the resultant uncertainty as to the ultimate level of prices is one of the greatest hindrances to business stability and development, and rising costs reduce purchases, particularly from overseas countries. Those who live on fixed incomes, pensioners, and those whose wages do not change with changes in the cost of living, endure hardship as the value of their money incomes continues to fall and prices rise. Even those who successfully make claims for wage increases find difficulty in keeping up with the rising cost of living because there is always a time lag between price rises and wage increases.

FALLING PRICES, if so marked as to constitute *deflation*, have depressing effects on economic activity; they are bad for trade. By reducing or destroying profit margins, they tend to discourage enterprise, restrict production, and to increase the volume of unemployment.

When prices are falling, goods already produced have

to be sold at lower prices than were anticipated when production was put in hand. Profits are, therefore, reduced
or completely fail to materialise, production is restricted,
wages become a heavier burden to industry, for they do
not fall as rapidly as prices (owing to the difficulty of
getting labour to accept lower rates of pay—wage rates,
as we saw above, always "lag" behind prices), overhead
charges per unit of output increase, costs of production
become greater relative to selling prices, plant has to be
left idle, unemployment ensues and dividends are reduced. In general, therefore, there is a fall in the general
purchasing power of the community, and the depression
extends throughout industry. Debts and interest payments become greater burdens at the very time when
producers are least able to carry them, and many failures
result.

But there is one section of the community that benefits. Those who receive fixed incomes can buy more at
the lower prices and their standard of living tends to
rise.

Price trends are generally in an upward direction and
rises have been particularly marked since the beginning
of the Second World War but rapid and marked changes
in the value of a currency, whether in an upward or
downward direction, are undesirable; they breed uncertainty and lead to widespread loss of confidence. International trade is hampered because the value of the currency cannot be estimated with any certainty, and buyers
and sellers in other countries are reluctant to enter into
transactions measured in terms of a currency of indefinite
and rapidly changing value.

INFLATION

Over a long period, the value of money has been falling, sometimes steadily and to a small extent, but at
times the fall has been rapid and marked as during the

two World Wars of this century when Governments resorted to heavy borrowing from the banks and from the public, and to extensive economic activity concentrated on the production of war equipment. With the increased demand for money to make payments to the Government's enlarged labour force and to its greater number of contractors, the volume of bank deposits increased markedly and more purchasing power became available. At the same time, there was a shortage of goods on which the consumer was able to spend his money. In such conditions, if maxima are not officially imposed on prices, prices rise. These inflationary conditions continued after the wars and the value of money continued to fall. The economic situation got out of hand, prices continued to rise, exports became too costly for overseas customers and balance of payments difficulties developed. Something had to be done to put the economic system on a sound and progressive basis; fiscal and financial measures were introduced involving the restriction of credit (the credit squeeze), and checking spending, both public and private.

Attempts at Government level have been made to curb inflation by restricting price and wage increases and trade unions have been asked to moderate the wage claims made for their members, only those being treated favourably which were related to increases in productivity. Firms and businesses also have been required to stabilise or reduce their prices.

BANKING

As the economic system has expanded and grown, the financial mechanism has become more complicated, credit transactions have enormously increased, and most business transactions of any magnitude now pass through the hands of the banks.

The Functions of a Bank

The British Banking System, in particular, is renowned for its high efficiency and for the variety of services it renders to the community. Originally, a bank was a place where people took their valuables for safe keeping; now it fulfils a number of other highly important functions. It *receives deposits* from customers on *current* account, *i.e.*, repayable on demand by cheque and bearing no interest, or on *deposit* account, repayable only after a period of notice and usually bearing interest; it *makes* fixed *loans* to its customers on loan account or gives them fluctuating *overdrafts* on current account; it *discounts* bills of exchange and promissory notes at market rates, and *accepts* bills of exchange on behalf of its customers and correspondents.

Most modern banks also undertake important *agency services* on behalf of their customers and other banks, as, for example, in the safe custody of valuables; in collecting cheques, dividends, coupons and foreign bills; in undertaking stock and share transactions and foreign exchange operations; and in carrying out the duties of attorney, executor, trustee, or referee as to the standing and integrity of customers.

The Utility of Banking to the Community

A consideration of the functions discussed in the preceding paragraphs will indicate at once that bankers render services of inestimable value to the trade and industry of the country. In acting as intermediaries between large numbers of depositors or lenders on the one hand and of equally numerous borrowers on the other, banks mobilise capital and make its use effective. They may be regarded as great reservoirs of loanable money into which flow a myriad of small streams of liquid funds, and from which are distributed throughout the country, at the times when they are most needed and in the places where they can be most efficiently used, supplies of capital which are rightly regarded as sources of further wealth. Countless small sums of money are rendered productive which would otherwise remain in "idle hoard", and in this way the banking organisation assists the transfer of the wealth of large and small capitalists in a rich locality to other areas where that wealth can be efficiently and profitably employed.

In general, the existence of a sound and well-developed banking system provides safety for small and large savings, enables payments to be made, even over great distances, with safety and dispatch, and so facilitates all types of financial operations. Hence, the existence of a sound and efficient banking system is in itself an encouragement to saving, thrift and economy. The small depositor is brought to appreciate the facilities for safe investment which the banks provide and thus we find that, in a modern community, even the lower income groups keep accounts at a savings bank or a joint stock bank.

CHEQUE CARDS

These cards add the credit of a bank to that of the drawer of the cheque; they thus increase the acceptability of the cheques and make them as good as cash. The cards are issued free and may be used for payments not exceeding £30. A cheque made out by the holder of a card within the specified amount will be honoured by any branch of the bank on which it is drawn or by a bank with which reciprocal arrangements have been made. Suppliers of goods and services are assured of payment if they accept cheques accompanied by cheque cards even if the customers are not known to them.

The British commercial banks (except Barclays Bank) using this service issue a standardised form of cheque card. Barclays Bank have their own special form of cheque card known as the *Barclaycard*.

CHAPTER IX

DISTRIBUTION OF THE PRODUCT OF INDUSTRY: RENT

OUR examination of the economic system up to this point has shown us why goods are produced, why services are performed, how the values of goods and services are determined, and how those values are measured in terms of money so as to facilitate the exchange of goods between producers and consumers. We have yet to consider how consumers obtain money with which they can in turn obtain control over some part of the total goods produced, *i.e.*, how they obtain the money with which to buy such goods as they require.

DISTRIBUTION

The branch of Economics that deals with this matter is known as *Distribution*. In the economic sense, Distribution means, not the physical transfer of goods and services, but the sharing out or apportionment of the total value of goods and services produced within a community during a given period among those who take part in their production, *i.e.*, among the factors of production, land, labour and capital; enterprise, too, must be rewarded.

These factors unite in any community to produce a sum total of goods and services, and each of these factors is, of course, entitled to a share of the aggregate value of those goods and services. This aggregate value is described by the Economist as the *National Income*, and is regarded as the net product of the fruits of industry that remains after allowances have been made for replacements of raw materials and depreciation of machinery during the period in which the Income is obtained, usually one year.

Our problem now is to discover what principles regulate the division of this net product of industry, or National Income, between the factors of production. The shares that go to land, labour, capital and enterprise are respectively known as *rent*, *wages*, *interest* and *profits*. Rent, however, in its economic sense, is applied to factors other than land.

The Nature of Rent

The term "rent" in Economics refers to the *payment made for the use of a factor of production the supply of which is fixed*. Its most frequent application is to the payment made for land.

The amount of the payment made in respect of any plot of land depends on demand and supply. The *total* supply of land is relatively fixed but some land is more desirable than other land and, therefore, in greater demand. Two properties of land affect the demand for any particular plot; its fertility and its situation.

In the case of land used for agricultural purposes, *fertility* is the main factor determining the demand for it. A farmer carefully considers the nature of the soil and the drainage of any plot of land he proposes to rent, and he will pay a higher rent for a more fertile plot than for a less fertile plot, because the more fertile plot is likely to give him a better return for his outlay of labour and capital.

The farmer also considers the *situation* of the land, and, other things being equal, he will choose land that is advantageously situated with regard to the prospective market for his produce. Usually he will pay a higher rent for land conveniently near a town or a railway station or a major road than for land far from a railway station, river or road and accessible only with difficulty.

If it is costly and troublesome to take food and necessary supplies to a farm, and difficult or expensive to convey produce from the farm to market, the rent that a farmer will be willing to pay for the farm will be relatively low.

In towns, where most of the land is used for the building of houses, shops, offices, factories and warehouses, or for roads, playing-fields, parks or recreation grounds, situation is of even greater importance. Land which is to be used for any such purposes need not be fertile; but it must be conveniently situated for the purpose for which it is required, *i.e.*, it must be *accessible*, and the more accessible it is the greater the demand and the higher the rent. So we find that rents in the centre of a city are higher than rents in the suburbs or in a nearby village.

Rent and Cost

Because land is scarce, there are competing uses for it, just as there are competing uses for any other factor of production. Factors of production can be used for any particular purpose only if they are withdrawn from other uses. They have, therefore, to be paid a reward at least equal to what they would have earned if they had been used in the production of something else.

In general, this applies to land just as much as to any other factor of production. The Classical Economists, of whom *David Ricardo* was probably the most eminent, treated land on a different basis, because they assumed that units of land can be used for one purpose only. If we assume that land can be used for wheat-growing alone, the only alternative to using it for that purpose is not using it at all.

But this is not so; inferior wheat-land may be excellent pasture-land, and as such may command a high rent. Again, land which cannot be used for growing wheat, may be profitably leased to a company which wants to build a golf-course or a residential estate on it. In practice, land can be, and is, transferred from one use to another whenever there is likely to be a gain from the transfer. Although the total supply of land is fixed, the supply of land *for any one use* can usually be increased, when the demand for its products rises, by diverting land from other uses.

Conversely, the supply of land for any particular use will be decreased if the demand for its product falls, by diverting some units to other uses.

Land has a real cost just like any other factor of production, *i.e.*, labour, capital or enterprise. One commodity can be produced only at the cost of withdrawing land from the production of other commodities. This real cost measures the rent that has in fact to be paid to obtain command over any unit of land. And the reward that has to be paid to a unit of land to divert it from some other use obviously enters into price. From the point of view of a particular industry, the cost of this unit is one that has to be met, otherwise no land will be forthcoming for that industry.

URBAN RENTS

Land which is more advantageously situated, *i.e.*, in reference to a market or railway station or centre of the city, or land that for any reason is more sought after, yields a higher rent than land not so advantageously situated. Rent in the suburbs of a large town is much higher than that in the surrounding agricultural areas, and there is a gradual increase as the centre of the town is approached.

The supply of land in exclusive London shopping centres such as Piccadilly and Bond Street is limited; sites in other parts of London cannot satisfy the same demand. Demand for the more central or more fashionable parts of any city is considerable and rents there are high, though high prices are not the effect of high rents; they are the cause. A shopkeeper in the West End of London is willing to pay a high rent because his customers are prepared to pay high prices for the privilege of shopping in an exclusive centre, or because, although selling prices may not be higher, his turnover will be large in such a district. High prices will be charged whatever the rent; landlords, as well as the tenants, know this, and competition between shop-keepers will, therefore, bring about high rents.

The payment made for the occupation of a dwelling is not pure rent. It consists largely of interest on the capital expended in the provision of the building and partly of an allowance for repairs and depreciation. Whilst, therefore, the land used for building purposes will yield its owner at least the current economic rent of agricultural land, payment for the occupation of a dwelling is not rent in the economic sense of the term. Rent in the economic sense is a payment solely for the use of land or other natural agent and does not include any return on capital invested.

Changes in Rent

Increases in the demand for certain types of produce will cause more land to be made available for their production, and the rent of the units concerned will rise. There will then be less land available for other uses, and other rents may rise as well.

If there is an increase of population or an advance in industrial technique that brings about a higher standard of living and so causes an increased demand for agricultural products in general, a uniform rise in rents is likely to take place. Conversely, a fall in population, or in the standard of living, will cause rents to fall.

Improvements in agricultural technique will have the effect of lowering rents in general. For although the improvements may affect only certain types of agricultural produce, they may enable a much greater output to be produced on less land. There will then be more land available for other purposes, so that other rents will fall as well. At the same time, it must be borne in mind that improved methods tend to benefit inferior units more than the more fertile ones. As new methods enable land that was previously not worth farming to be brought under cultivation, the rent of inferior units may rise. Although rents in general may be lower, the effect of inventions may be to even up rents over different plots of land.

A reduction in costs of transport will raise the rents of previously inaccessible land. That does not mean that the rents of intra-marginal land will be increased in proportion. On the contrary, they are more likely to fall as the result of competition from more distant sources of supply.

RENT OF ABILITY

Units of labour, like units of land, differ from other units. Some barristers are very successful while others have to work hard to make ends meet; some artists achieve success and sell their services, pictures, etc., at high prices while others have difficulty in finding buyers at all. The successful people earn high rewards because they are the possessors of special talents and the supply of such talents is relatively fixed. The earnings gained as a result of the possession of such unique talents are a true rent, a rent of ability.

UNEARNED INCREMENT

When the value of land rises quite independently of the investment of labour and capital in the land, as, for example, because of growth of population (in towns) or as the result of the building of a railway or of a major road, an *"unearned increment"* is said to accrue to the property-owner. This return is unearned in the sense that the owners of the land have done nothing to bring about the additional value acquired by the land, and for this reason such additions to land values are regarded as suitable for taxation, or appropriation by the State.

ROYALTIES

A royalty is the payment made by the operator of a mine or oil-well to the mineowner or land-owner. Usually, this payment is fixed for a long period ahead on an estimate, made by a surveyor, of the resources of the mine or well and of its annual output during that period.

A royalty differs from a rent. A rent is a payment made for the use of the *indestructible* powers of the soil. The land is not injured when cultivated or used for pasture; in fact, it is generally improved. Mining and oil production, on the other hand, deprive the land of part of its riches; once coal and oil, tin and gold, are taken out of the land they cannot be restored, so the value of the land is correspondingly reduced. A royalty, therefore, is partly a rent and *partly a compensation for the decrease in the value of the land* caused by the removal of part of its mineral wealth.

THE JUSTIFICATION FOR THE PAYMENT OF RENT

The proposal for nationalisation can be better justified in the case of land than it can in the case of other factors of production. Clearly, as things stand at present, we have to face a slow but certain rise in rents as land gradually becomes more scarce. This rise in rents is in no way due to the efforts of landowners; it is a type of *unearned* income.

At the same time, the recipients of rent, *i.e.*, the owners of land, are as justly entitled to their income as are the recipients of interest, for in the vast majority of cases they have invested their money in land as an income-yielding security. To deprive them of that income would be quite as unfair as to abolish the payment of interest on Government stocks. It would be a direct negation of the rights of private property. The owner of land is fully entitled to draw a payment for its use, in the same way as the possessor of a collection of rare pictures is entitled to any income he can obtain by exhibiting them. But as against this there is the view that rent of land arises from social causes over which no one individual has control and for which no individual can claim credit, as he can in regard to other forms of income.

CHAPTER X

WAGES, THE REWARD OF LABOUR

MOST people receive their share of the product of industry in the form of "wages", which term is used in Economics to denote any form of remuneration for labour or for service. The bricklayer, the bus driver, the shop assistant, the teacher, the bank clerk, the doctor, the solicitor, and a host of other people receive wages as the reward for contributing to production by their efforts, mental or manual, of "hand" or of "brain". Though in certain grades of society these rewards are given the more dignified name of *salary* or *fee* or *emolument*, their nature is the same as that of wages and no different principle is involved in their determination.

METHODS OF WAGE PAYMENT

The two chief methods of payment for labour are *Time Wages* and *Piece Wages*.

TIME WAGES are paid for a certain length of labour-time—an hour, a day, a week, a month or a year. This method is general in those occupations, such as transport, clerical work and agriculture, where it is difficult or impossible to measure the quantity and quality of the work, or where the work varies greatly between different workers; and also in those occupations where careful application is required and undue haste might cause loss or damage to the product or to the tools or machinery used, *e.g.*, in artistic work, or in high-class millinery or in diamond-cutting.

Where time rates of wages are paid, much depends on the honesty and loyalty of the worker, or alternatively on the effectiveness of supervision. Whether he works fast or slowly, well or badly, he is paid the agreed rate of wages. Usually the time worker is doing work that he likes and can do well, while the employer, appreciating this fact, relies upon his doing his best and pays him accordingly.

PIECE WAGES take the form of a specified payment for a certain unit of output; e.g., so many pence for pressing a suit of clothes or for mending a pair of shoes, or for addressing 1,000 envelopes, or for turning a brass fitting. By this method, the worker is paid according to what he produces; the faster he works, the more units he completes and the more he receives. There is, consequently, a tendency to scamped and imperfect work. Hence this system can be adopted only in those industries where individual output can be easily and quickly measured and inspected, as in the shirt-making, boot and shoe and metal-working industries, where the products are usually standardised.

In practice, piece rates and time rates must have reference to each other. Piece rates can be fixed only when it is known approximately how long a worker earning a certain wage will take to do a certain job or produce a given article. Piece rates also must be so adjusted that a certain minimum day-wage is earned: they would obviously be unacceptable to the worker if they were fixed so low as not to enable him to earn a reasonable wage, whilst they might be ruinous to the employer if they were fixed too high. On the other hand, a time rate must be based, directly or indirectly, on the average amount of work that can be done or is likely to be done in a specified time.

REAL WAGES

The wage paid to the worker, however calculated, is by no means a true indicator of his economic position. The worker who tells us he earns £15 a week has not told

us all. To have a true picture of his earnings we must
know many other things. We must know if his work is
irregular or regular, pleasant or unpleasant, the length of
his working day, the nature of his employment, its effect
on his health and strength, *i.e.*, whether his working life
is likely to be long or short, the prospects of success, and
whether there is a possibility of adding to his earnings by
overtime or spare-time work.

To judge whether a worker's earnings are high or low,
we must also know something of the purchasing power of
money. A money income of £15 earned at a time when, or
in a place where, food and other things are very cheap
represents a higher *real* wage than £15 earned at a time
when, or in a place where, food and other essentials are
extremely dear.

*A man's real income consists of the net advantages he
obtains from his employment.* Some workers are paid
partly in kind; thus the steward of a club, in addition
to his wage, usually receives free quarters, heating,
lighting and possibly even free food. Other workers may
have special facilities for purchasing the commodities
they help to sell or to produce, *e.g.*, shop assistants may
be allowed a discount on their purchases in the shop
where they work; the miner gets coal for nothing or at
low prices; the railwayman receives free or cheap passes
for railway travelling both for himself and for his family;
workers in large departmental stores and catering firms
can get their food and other articles at favourable prices.
In some jobs, too, extra income can be earned in spare
time, as in the case of a school-teacher, who can take
private pupils or evening classes after ordinary school
hours. A clerical worker may receive a lower money
wage than a manual worker, but usually his work is
cleaner and less arduous.

In addition to such special cases, we must remember
when we consider the *real* income of many members of

the community that they receive a *welfare income* from the provision of social services by the State and municipalities, *e.g.*, free education for their children, and social security benefits during ill-health, unemployment and on retirement.

DIFFERENCES IN WAGES

When we have allowed for these factors, we can make a reasonable estimate of the value of a man's *real* wages. But we are not, even then, in a position to know why wages vary as between different industries and even in the same industry in different parts of the country. Why, for example, is the farm labourer paid less than the carpenter? Why do skilled men normally receive higher wages than unskilled men? Why are printers in London paid more than printers in the provinces?

When we consider these differences, we see at once that Society values the work of one man more highly than that of another; we see that the community pays relatively little to a dustman, but gives a high rate of pay to a skilled surgeon or a successful lawyer. Within a trade, differences in personal ability may easily account for differences in wages; we should expect the more skilful tailor working on piece rates to earn more than his less skilful colleague, but this does not explain differences of wages *as between different trades*.

To solve this problem we have to discover how the wages of particular groups of workers are determined.

THE RELATION BETWEEN WAGES AND MARGINAL PRODUCTIVITY

The wage of labour, *i.e.*, the value of labour, is, like all other values, determined according to the general laws of supply and demand. Wages tend to a level where the demand for labour and the supply of labour are in equilibrium. If at any moment, the wage rate for a given type of labour is high, the demand for that labour will tend to fall and the supply of people who can do the work will tend to increase: more people will try to get into the trade. If, on the other hand, wage rates in a given trade are low, people will leave the trade for some other occupation, whilst employers will tend to employ more workmen in order to reap the benefit of the low rates prevailing.

On the demand side (*i.e.*, the employer's side), wages are determined by the *marginal productivity of labour*. With labour, as with other factors of production, the yield or productivity of each additional unit employed in any kind of production decreases after a certain point is reached (this can be compared with the Law of Diminishing Utility).

Let us consider an employer taking on men to work in his factory. After a point, each additional man employed adds a smaller quantity to the total output than the previous employee, and a stage is reached when the last worker employed adds only just as much to the *value* of the total output as the wages he is paid. Clearly it is not worth the employer's while to take on any more men after this "marginal" worker. Since the employer pays equal wages to all workers in a given grade, it follows that the wages of all the workers in any grade of labour equal the *marginal productivity* of that labour, *i.e.*, the value of the additional output obtained by the employment of the last labourer just worth employing.

Competition between employers for a given supply of labour brings about this equilibrium between wages and the marginal productivity of the number employed. The demand for labour of a particular grade is determined by the total demands of all employers. If the wage rate is below the marginal productivity of the labour force of any employer, it will pay him to take on more men. Each employer will, therefore, try to employ that number for which the marginal productivity is equal to the wage ruling. Now if this total demand exceeds the supply of labour being offered at that wage, competition between employers will raise the wage rate. Alternatively, if the supply of labour exceeds the demand for it at a given wage, the wage rate will fall owing to competition between workers seeking employment.

The principle of marginal productivity does not imply that an employer will dismiss men or take on more men as soon as there is a divergence between wages and marginal productivity. For one thing, it is not easy to measure marginal productivity at any time. Again, the dismissal of men may result in disorganisation of the business. Marginal productivity is a *guide* to the employer as to when it will be profitable for him to make a change in his labour force. The speed with which he acts will depend on the circumstances.

The direction of labour might be controlled in order to improve the national economy or in an emergency. Certain industries are given priority in wartime and labour is withdrawn from consumer goods industries such as furniture making and directed to munition making.

The Worker's Standard of Life

On the supply side (the worker's side), there is a minimum wage that the worker will accept. This minimum represents the cost of maintaining his customary *standard of life, i.e.*, the amount of necessaries, comforts and luxuries he is accustomed to enjoy and upon which he will, in the long run, insist under conditions of free competition. Although, by reason of the action of employers, wages *in the short run* will tend to equal the marginal productivity of the labour employed, *in the long run* wages must also be sufficient to maintain the standard of life to which the workers are accustomed, otherwise the supply of that kind of labour will tend to fall off. Workers will leave the trade and try something else, and young people will not be encouraged to enter it.

THE DETERMINATION OF WAGES

Wages *tend* to fall to a point at which there will be a demand for all the labour seeking employment. In those grades where there is overcrowding (as, for instance, in unskilled occupations), the worker tends to receive low wages because marginal productivity, as measured by the relation between the demand for labour and its supply, tends to be low; and in those industries where the supply of labour, relative to the demand, is scarce, wages are high because marginal productivity is high.

We can now see why skilled men usually receive higher wages than unskilled men. The reason is that the intensity of the demand for the services of skilled men, relative to the available supply, is greater than the intensity of the demand for unskilled workers relative to their supply. In other words, the marginal productivity of skilled men exceeds that of unskilled men.

WAGE DIFFERENCES REFLECT NET ADVANTAGES WHERE COMPETITION IS FREE

The differences in the wages of various groups of workers are, therefore, mainly attributable to the relation between the demand for the labour of each group and the size of each group, *i.e.*, the supply of labour in that group. If competition were perfectly free, wage differences would reflect the differences in the *net advantages of each occupation*, and these net advantages would be determined by the factors we have already considered in discussing real wages, *e.g.*, the pleasantness of the occupation, prospects of success, and the length of the working day. Any disparity between wage rates and net advantages would be corrected by labour movements from one form of occupation to another.

The facts, however, are that competition is not

perfectly free, and that entry to certain occupations is restricted because considerable expense had to be incurred in acquiring the necessary knowledge and skill, and in the period of waiting before earnings or fees come in (*e.g.*, in the case of a doctor or barrister or solicitor). These barriers are, normally, strong enough to prevent the influx into such occupations of recruits sufficient in number to lower the marginal productivity of that kind of labour to a level equal to that of unskilled labourers. In occupations where entry is not difficult because little skill is required (*e.g.*, labourers), the supply available is usually so great as to result in low marginal productivity. Thus, there are relatively few doctors, because the expense of training cannot be borne by many; but there are relatively many labourers, because the work requires little skill.

Skilled men do not earn high wages because they have acquired the skill necessary to their occupations; they earn high wages because the acquiring of that skill has limited their supply. Unskilled men receive low wages not because their occupations need no skill, but because the absence of skill allows their supply to increase readily. A wage-rate measures the value of labour, and value is a rate of exchangeability, not an inherent property of the thing valued. It can, therefore, properly be understood only in terms of demand relative to supply. Were doctors as numerous as labourers *in relation to the demand for their services*, their remuneration would be at a low level. Conversely, were labourers as scarce as doctors relative to the demand for their services, the wages of a labourer would be high, although the work is unskilled.

In a time of depression, dustmen may be receiving higher wages than many skilled engineers, because the demand for engineers, relative to the supply, is small. As a rule, a depression in industry, and intense competition in engineering from countries where the standard of living and level of wages are low, will affect engineering very seriously. In such conditions there may be, relatively, little demand for engineers, and their wages will fall to a very low level. The demand for dustmen, on the other hand, is not subject to the fluctuations of industry or to international competition; municipal service is a *sheltered* industry, and dustmen get much the same wage whether trade generally is good or bad. Engineers, on the other hand, earn high wages, but suffer from unemployment or shorter working time when there is little trade activity.

WHY ARE WOMEN'S WAGES USUALLY LOWER THAN MEN'S?

The principle of marginal productivity thus enables us to understand why some men earn less than other men. It also enables us to understand why women, as a rule, earn lower wages than men. The plain fact is that all occupations are not open to men and women equally. Physical, legal and conventional barriers operate to confine women to a relatively small range of occupations. This means that in many occupations open to women the supply of labour is relatively great and marginal productivity is consequently low. Low marginal productivity, as we have seen, means low wages. The coalminer's sister who works as a shop assistant does not earn lower wages than her brother because she is not physically able to hew coal. The fact is that the supply of shop assistants, relative to the demand, is normally greater than the supply of miners relative to the demand.

EQUAL PAY FOR EQUAL WORK

"Equal pay for equal work" is an expression of the claim that the same wages should be paid for the same work. Usually, equality applies as between men in the same trade, thanks very largely to the efforts of trade

unions: but it is more difficult to get wage equality as
between men and women even in the same trade.

The problem bristles with difficulties, because it is not
always easy to say what is equal work. Even where
similar clerical work is being performed by a man and a
woman, it is not certain that they are equally useful to
the employer. The employer may have greater faith in
the man's ability to cope with an emergency situation, or
in his greater immunity from illness, or in his greater
ability to stand the strain of busy periods. Men will
work under conditions that would be unsuitable for a
woman, and they can be called upon to undertake jobs
that an employer would hesitate to give to a woman.
Women, too, may leave their employment on marriage,
though there is now a large and growing number of
women who remain at work after marriage or return to
work when their children go to school.

In many cases there can be little doubt that the work
is equal, *e.g.*, among piece-workers in textile and clothing
trades. In such cases, therefore, there is equal pay for
equal work, and the employer is indifferent whether he
employs men or women for the jobs in question.

Where the value of the employee to the employer
cannot be so easily ascertained as in piece-work, the
lower wage paid to the woman for apparently the same
work as the man must be due to the fact that the employer considers she is worth less. And it follows that
women are then employed because their services *can* be
obtained at a lower wage than is paid to men.

The claim of equal pay for equal work is often merely
a claim for raising women's wages to the level of men's
wages. If the principle were generally adopted, the
rate of women's wages would, in most cases, be in excess
of their marginal worth to the employer. The result
would be that, provided an adequate supply of male
labour were available, many women would be dismissed

and their places taken by men, for, at the higher wage, the employer would prefer men to women. To the extent that there were unemployed men who could do the women's work, unemployment amongst men would decrease and unemployment amongst women increase.

The increased unemployment amongst women would swell the number seeking work in occupations in which they do not compete with men, and in these occupations there would be a tendency for women's wages to fall. Recognition of the right of women to equal pay for equal work was emphasised by the *Equal Pay Act* 1970 which prevents discrimination between men and women as regards the terms and conditions of employment.

TRADE UNIONS AND WAGES

A TRADE UNION is a continuous association of wage-earners for the purpose of maintaining or improving their economic position, and, in this and certain other countries, such unions exert a considerable influence on wages and working conditions. The earliest associations were *craft unions*, in which membership was restricted to those who followed a particular craft, *e.g.*, weaving or masonry. Next in point of time came the *industrial union*, embracing all those in an industry or service, *e.g.*, coal-mining and railway transport. Later came the *"general" workers' union*, embracing unskilled, semi-skilled and general workers in many miscellaneous industries, *e.g.*, dock labourers and road workers. All three types are represented in our present-day labour organisation; the *Amalgamated Society of Woodworkers* is a craft union, the *National Union of Railwaymen* is an industrial union and the *Transport and General Workers' Union* is a general union.

The extent to which trade unions can influence wages depends on the operation of two powerful factors: *the elasticity of demand for the product* and the *proportion that wage costs bear to total costs*. If the product is one for which demand is elastic, that is, if a small rise in price leads to a large fall in demand, and if wage costs form a high proportion of the total cost of its production, the power of trade unions to raise wages in the industry concerned is severely limited, because any increase in wages will force up costs and prices, and these higher prices will lead to a serious curtailment of demand. The result will be unemployment of trade union members.

Wages, then, cannot be lastingly increased beyond what the industry can afford to pay. The trade union can raise wages in any particular industry to the level justified by the workers' marginal productivity where wages up to that level are not already being paid. *During short periods*, a strong trade union may force up wages beyond this level, but this can be done only at the expense of profits, or of the consumer. If profits are reduced below the normal level, enterprise and capital will shun the industry; if prices are raised, the effect on the consumer will depend on the nature of the demand for the product, as explained above.

Ultimately, therefore, wages depend on the efficiency of the industry. A trade union can improve that efficiency, but its real effect on wages depends on its ability to secure *equal pay for equal work* performed by its members. Trade unions have been effective both in raising the general rate of wages and in standardising the rates paid throughout the whole of an industry, and so preventing individual exploitation.

A trade union can ensure that the workers get their fair share of the product as measured by their marginal productivity. If an industry improves in prosperity, the union can demand a portion of the increase for the workers; but if an industry does not prosper, higher wages cannot permanently be paid, however strong the union.

TRADE UNIONS AND HOURS

The increased nervous strain caused by the general speeding up of production and the development of the machine system of industry led to the intensification of the workers' demand for reduced hours. At the same time, the essential monotony of modern industrial life and the increasing claims of politics, literature, the arts, and sport upon the interest of the workers, all increase the tendency to demand more leisure.

On psychological and moral grounds the case for a shorter day might be justified even though it involved an economic loss, but many investigations show that often the case for reduced hours of labour has an economic justification. It has been shown that, when hours are shortened, economies of production are generally effected: overstrain is eliminated, accidents are reduced, and generally the fixed capital of industry is used more economically, so that losses and expenses are diminished and output tends to increase at less cost per unit.

Recognition of the economic benefits to the worker of adequate leisure lies behind the arrangements made in many industries for the statutory fixing of "holidays with pay". Also, voluntary agreements operate in many industries and occupations not covered by statute. Practically all wage-earners in Britain are now covered by agreements or orders for holidays with pay.

INDUSTRIAL RELATIONS

To ensure continuity of production, disrupted by strikes, lockouts and unsatisfactory relations between employees and employers, the *Industrial Relations Act* 1971 was passed. This Act set up the *National Industrial Relations Court* and the *Registry of Trade Unions and Associations of Employers*. All trade unions and associations of employers are required to register.

CHAPTER XI

INTEREST, THE RETURN TO CAPITAL

INTEREST is the payment made for the use of capital by the borrower of capital to the lender. It is the amount paid by a borrower of capital over and above the original sum borrowed. If a customer borrows £1,000 from his bank for a year at 5 per cent., he will, at the end of the year, pay the bank £1,050. The additional £50 is the interest paid by the customer for borrowing the £1,000 for one year. Interest is usually calculated annually as a percentage of the original amount borrowed, and this percentage is known as the *rate of interest*.

In examining the theory of interest, we are confronted with two problems. The first, *Why is interest paid?* And the second, *What determines the rate of interest?*

Before we approach these problems we must understand clearly what we mean by "the rate of interest", for in any community there are in existence at the same time many different rates of interest. In this country, for instance, we may lend our money to the State by putting it in Government Stock and get one rate, or we may put it on deposit in a commercial bank and get another. We may get even higher rates if we invest the money in a building society or lend it on mortgage or invest it in the debentures of a company.

GROSS INTEREST

Clearly, different types of borrowers pay different rates of interest. Our Government and the Governments of other great Powers can borrow at relatively low rates of interest, whilst gold-mining and oil-producing companies, whose operations are known to involve considerable risk of loss of the capital used, may pay high rates to induce people to lend them the money needed to exploit their mines and oilfields. Again, the yield we may get by investing our money in the debentures of a British manufacturing company may be only 12 per cent., whereas we may obtain as much as 20 per cent. on debentures issued by a copper-mining company. We may find, too, that while our local bank is charging its customers 7 per cent. for an advance, a moneylender in the same street may be getting as much as 20 per cent. from the people who resort to him.

The reason for this variation in the payment made by borrowers to lenders of capital is that the total return or *gross interest* received by the lenders includes certain elements in addition to net interest, viz., (1) *a payment for the risk of losing the capital lent;* and (2) *a payment for the trouble and inconvenience entailed in looking after the investment.*

If we lend our money to the British Government by putting it in the Post Office Savings Bank, we know that it is as safe as it is normally possible to make it, and we are therefore content with a low rate of interest. If we lend our money to a rubber- or oil- or gold-producing company, we know that we are running a degree of risk that we shall lose the whole or part of our capital, and we require a high rate to induce us to invest in such concerns.

Some investments, again, require a good deal of attention, and investors watch the market continuously. The investor needs to satisfy himself that there is as little risk as possible of his investment depreciating (through a fall in its quotation on the stock exchange), or of interest or dividend not being paid. Fluctuating fortunes of the particular company, or of industry in general, will affect dividends and share-quotations, so that the latter tend to vary more widely than in the case of Government stock. In consequence, many investors prefer a relatively low but safe return from Government stock to a higher but more speculative yield from shares of commercial undertakings.

NET INTEREST

The factors of risk and trouble, therefore, account for differences in the rates of gross interest in different contracts between borrowers and lenders. But when allowance has been made for them, there remains a *minimum* or *net rate of interest* which even the most secure and fluid investment must pay, at a given time, in order to attract the capital it requires. This *net* or *pure* rate of interest is the payment made solely for the use of capital, as distinct from any risk or trouble that may be involved by the investment. In practice, such a rate may be taken as that received on Government stock, in which it may be assumed there is little element of risk or inconvenience.

This minimum rate tends to be equal for all borrowers. Rates of gross interest may vary widely at any given time as between different borrowers, but net or pure interest must be the same for all borrowers, because there can be only one price in the same market, at any particular time, for the same commodity—the commodity in this case being capital. Competition for capital between different borrowers and the mobility of capital between different investments ensure equality in the rate of net interest over the whole range of investments. And *as between those investments that involve approximately the same inconvenience and the same risk, the rates of gross interest tend also to be equal.*

WHY IS INTEREST PAID?

To understand why interest is paid at all, we must obtain a clear conception of the service performed by capital in production. It has already been explained that capital consists of real things—machines, plant, raw material and factories—or resources that can be converted into such things. Such things are not free to all. They are owned only by certain individuals, or can be obtained only by those who have command over the necessary means of exchange. Like other things that are scarce and in demand, therefore, capital *commands a price*, and that price is interest. Without capital, production could not be carried on, so the producer who wants capital must pay for it in the same way as he pays for labour or for land.

If a manufacturer or other business man has to hire a machine (*e.g.*, a calculating machine), we should expect him to pay for it, and if he decided to borrow money in order to buy that machine, we should expect him to pay for the hire of the money that makes the purchase possible.

Although it thus seems only reasonable and equitable to us that people should pay for the use of capital, the ancient Greek and Roman philosophers regarded the payment of interest as unjustifiable, and in the Middle Ages the Church went so far as to forbid *usury*—the lending of money at interest. This attitude was due partly to the fact that there was in those days little use for hired capital, and partly to the fact that money was lent only to accommodate the unfortunate, often with baneful control by the lender over the borrower.

When industry and commerce developed, however, there arose a legitimate demand for the use of capital by enterprising producers; gradually the payment of interest came to be tolerated, and eventually it was regarded as justified and even necessary. It was recognised that a properly conducted business transaction for the loan of money for productive purposes was of advantage to both lender and borrower, and that borrowed capital, when used by the producer in conjunction with the other factors of production, was creative of productive resources. It came to be realised that the owner of capital lent to producers was justly entitled to a part of the increase in resources made possible by the use of his capital, and that interest paid for the use of capital was a justifiable recompense for the capitalist's abstention from the immediate enjoyment which his capital could make possible.

BORROWERS PAY INTEREST BECAUSE CAPITAL IS PRODUCTIVE

Borrowers are willing to pay interest on borrowed capital, therefore, because by means of it they gain command over goods and services from the use of which they benefit. Nowadays, the majority of loans are made to assist production. By using borrowed capital, producers can buy machines and raw material, erect buildings and hire labour, and with the assistance of such factors can produce commodities worth considerably more than the sum of money borrowed.

Capital is needed, moreover, because production takes time—there is a time interval between the buying of plant and raw materials and the hiring of labour, and the appearance of the finished article on the market. Only when the article is sold does the producer get back the money he has spent. To tide over the interval, the producer must either himself have saved money, or he must induce somebody who has saved to lend him the money. If he has no savings himself, the fact that he can obtain command over real resources by using someone else's savings means that he can set in motion productive processes from which he expects to derive a gain. Producers are, therefore, quite ready to pay a lender part of the product obtained by the use of his capital, for they can produce not only sufficient to pay for the loan, but also sufficient to repay themselves for their own efforts and organisation. Thus capital shares in the product of industry because it co-operates with the other factors of production in turning out that product. In brief, *borrowers pay interest for the use of capital because capital is productive*.

LENDERS GET INTEREST AS AN INDUCEMENT TO SAVE

The lender, on his part, expects to be reimbursed for the service he performs. Owners of capital might not be willing to postpone enjoyment of their capital if they were not adequately compensated for their sacrifice. It is not enough that they will get their capital back in the future; *the majority of lenders must be compensated for being deprived of its immediate use*. Most people would prefer to spend rather than to save, and so require something to induce them to save rather than to spend. To most of us, the present is so much more real than the future that we are inclined to let the future take care of itself.

Interest is therefore the inducement that is offered to get people to save capital. It is obvious that some people save without the inducement of interest. Many people put their savings in a bank regardless of the interest received. But such savings would not provide enough capital to satisfy all requirements. It is, in fact, the competition between borrowers for the limited supply of capital that is available that causes a price to be paid for it. And as there is only one price for the same commodity in the capital market, as there is in other markets, the same price is paid to all lenders by borrowers of a given class, even though some lenders might have saved without the incentive of that price.

THE FUNCTION OF THE RATE OF INTEREST

Since the supply of capital is limited, the rate of interest fulfils an important function in directing the limited supply into the channels where it can be most profitably used. The rate of interest is, so to speak, *an automatic regulator of the distribution of capital.* Those who can use capital most profitably offer the highest price for it and, consequently, they have a better chance of obtaining what is available; those who have little or no use for additional capital will pay little or nothing to get hold of it and, therefore, little of the available capital comes into their hands.

Suppose, for example, that capital is wanted for building cinemas and ice-skating rinks, but that the outlook for cinemas at the time in question is brighter than the outlook for ice-skating rinks. Clearly, the prospective cinema proprietor will offer a higher rate of interest for the loan of capital than the man who wants to build an ice-skating rink, with the result that available supplies of capital are diverted to cinema construction, and the ice-skating business has to wait.

The prevailing rate of interest, therefore, has a rationing effect; and when we read that an industry is unable to obtain sufficient capital, we may presume that the prospects of profitable employment of capital in that industry are not as bright as the prospects elsewhere, and that the industry concerned is not able to offer a rate of gross interest high enough to overcome the disinclination of investors to put their money into it.

WHAT DETERMINES THE RATE OF INTEREST?

Like other prices, the price paid for the use of capital, *i.e.,* the rate of interest, is determined by the relation between the demand for capital and its supply.

THE SUPPLY OF CAPITAL depends on the ability and

willingness of people to make present sacrifices, *i.e.*, on the *power* and *will* of people to *save*. The power to save is a social matter, the will to save is more personal.

The Power to Save depends mainly upon the general efficiency of industry. If the "net product" of industry increases because of the greater efficiency of one or some of the factors of production—land, labour, capital or enterprise—the owners of these factors will have a greater return in the form of rent, wages, interest and profit, and consequently a larger margin out of which to save.

There are, however, many other factors that influence the magnitude of the product out of which savings can be made, as, for example, the extent of the natural resources of the country, the use made of those resources, the soundness of the financial policy of the Government, the efficiency of the credit system of the country and the extent and profitableness of the nation's foreign trade.

Although China, for example, has large cereal and copper resources, they are not fully developed, and contribute less to her National Income than do the coal resources of Britain, or of Germany, or of the United States, to the National Incomes of those countries. Again, the stability of Britain's political and financial institutions has enabled her to develop her natural resources to a much greater extent than has been possible in underdeveloped countries where political security and financial resources have yet to be acquired.

The Will to Save depends on many personal factors, such as foresight, or anxiety about the future; the desire to provide for old age and for the education of children; the degree of personal and national security, without which saving is useless; the social esteem and power that the possession of wealth engenders; the tenacity of the "habit of work"; the available facilities for safe and profitable investment; and the inducement afforded by the prevailing rate of interest. Generally, the higher the rate of interest, the greater the will to save; but this is not always the case, because some people have so much wealth that they could not reasonably spend all they possess, even if the rate of interest was so low as to afford them no inducement to save.

The will to save cannot, however, be regarded as having a direct influence on the supply of capital in the sense that an increase in the will to save automatically leads to an increase in the supply of capital, and *vice versa.* Even though people decide to save more, that does not mean that the total savings of the community increase. The fact that some people save more may well result in less being saved by others. This will come about in the following way. If people decide to spend less on consumption, the immediate effect will be that dealers are left with unsold stocks. They will, therefore, place smaller orders for replacements. Production will consequently fall, the incomes of those engaged in production will fall, and at the lower level of incomes, the power to save may be smaller than before. Conversely, a decreased desire to save, accompanied by an increase in spending, may stimulate production, increase incomes, and so increase the power to save.

Changes in the will to save may, therefore, have the opposite effect from the one anticipated. Only if the amount saved is invested, so that new incomes can be created as a result of the investment, and so that production and incomes need not fall, will changes in the will to save and in the power to save go hand in hand.

THE DEMAND FOR CAPITAL depends on the marginal productivity of capital. The use or application of capital in production is influenced, as with the other factors of production, by the operation of the Law of Diminishing Returns. As more capital is applied to a given quantity of land and labour, the successive investments are less and less productive, so *the producer aims at using capital up to that point where its marginal productivity is equal to the rate of interest paid.*

Suppose, for example, that a manufacturer intent on extending his business is undecided whether to borrow £10,000, or £20,000, or £30,000. He may assess the utility or productivity to him of a first £10,000 at 7 per cent., the utility of an additional £10,000 at 5 per cent., the utility of a still further £10,000 at 4 per cent., and so on. The amount he borrows (*i.e.*, his demand for capital) depends on the rate of interest at which he can get the capital. If the rate in the market is 4 per cent., he will probably borrow £30,000; if it is 5 per cent., he will borrow £20,000, and if it is 7 per cent., he will borrow only £10,000.

The aggregate of the demands for capital at various rates by all borrowers constitutes the total demand for capital. If, at a given rate, the total demand of borrowers is less than the total supply, competition between lenders causes the rate to fall. If, on the other hand, the demand for capital at any rate is greater than the supply, competition between borrowers causes the rate to rise to a level where the supply of capital is equal to the demand. The determination of the rate of interest in the capital market is thus seen to follow the same process as the determination of any other market price.

It has already been explained that if a certain supply of a commodity was required by the community, it would not be forthcoming unless the price offered in the market was high enough to cover the marginal cost of that supply. In the same way, we can say that a *given supply of capital will not be forthcoming unless the rate of interest is high enough to bring into use the last portion of capital needed*, and this will be the capital owned by the most reluctant investor. He is called the *marginal investor*, and the interest he requires is analogous to marginal cost of production in the case of commodities.

The rate of interest on a given supply of capital, therefore, must be high enough to tempt the marginal investor, *i.e.*, the investor who is on the margin of doubt whether the rate of interest is a sufficient compensation to him for postponing the immediate use of his capital. If the rate offered is lower than this, the investor on the margin will prefer to spend now, rather than wait for the future enjoyment of his money, and the lower the prevailing rate of interest, the less capital will be offered for investment. Investors may be reluctant to invest because their *liquidity preference* is high; they prefer to have their assets in readily realisable form so that they can draw on them when necessary. Money is the most liquid of all resources and thus liquidity preference is a preference to hold money rather than to invest.

When the supply of capital is equated with the demand, the rate of net interest that causes such an equilibrium is the rate that is just sufficient to induce the most unwilling of the contributors of that supply of capital to bring forth their supply. Suppose, for example, that £10,000 of capital is required, and that £9,900 can be obtained at 5 per cent., but that the other £100 is not forthcoming unless the rate is 6 per cent. The owners of this £100 will be the marginal investors relative to a supply of £10,000, and—as only one rate of net interest can exist in any market at the same time—*the rate paid to them must be paid to all. The rate of interest applicable to all capital is thus governed by the rate that must be paid to the marginal investor whose contribution completes the total supply required.*

INTEREST AND COST OF PRODUCTION

As interest is paid by the producer for the hire of a factor of production, it is part of the cost of production, and, in the long run, it must be covered by the normal price of the product. Interest is a contractual payment:

the producer has to arrange the rate of interest on the capital he borrows before he begins to use that capital in production, and he must pay the agreed rate of interest to the lender irrespective of whether a profit is made or not. But if the producer did not anticipate a sufficient return to enable him to meet the interest on his borrowings, he would not have contracted to pay interest; and if he cannot earn enough with the capital he borrows to cover payment of the interest demanded by the lenders, he will have to curtail his borrowing or cease borrowing altogether.

INTEREST IS INEVITABLE

The Economist maintains that capital yields interest, whether it is owned by individuals, by corporations or by the State itself, because it is used productively. If all the capital in the country were owned by the State, interest would still accrue as a result of the productive employment of that capital. Therefore, the ownership of capital cannot affect the fact that it earns a return in the form of interest, and consequently the Socialist objection to the control of capital by individuals is not a valid objection to the payment of interest for the use of capital.

On the other hand, there is some justification for the claim of Socialists that the payment of interest provides the capitalist with an income for which he has not worked. The capitalist merely *allows* his capital to be used, and, even if he has laboured to amass that capital, it is still true that he obtains interest without working for it, because the reward for his past labour was the capital itself.

But if the system of private property is to be maintained, and if it is recognised that capital is an essential factor in production, then it appears reasonable to conclude that nothing should be done that would tend to interfere with the adequate supply of that factor. *The inducement to possess capital depends essentially on the recognition of private ownership and on the possibility of obtaining an income from accumulated capital in return for its use.* So long as private ownership of property is recognised, it is clear that some reward in the form of interest must be paid if the services of capital in production are to be continued and encouraged, and it must be left to competitive forces to ensure that the rate of remuneration of capital is not in excess of the economic service that it renders.

SAVE AS YOU EARN

To encourage national savings and so expand investments (urgently needed for industrial expansion) a contractual savings scheme was introduced in Britain in 1969. The "Save as you earn" scheme (S.A.Y.E.) is operated by trustee savings banks and building societies, and a national scheme is run by the Department for National Savings. Regular amounts, within specified limits, are saved by means of deductions from earnings made by employers or by payments made by contributors and, provided the savings have been completed and there have been no withdrawals, the savings qualify for a bonus equal to one year's savings free of tax at the end of five years and for a double bonus at the end of seven years, *i.e.*, two years' savings free of tax.

CHAPTER XII

PROFITS, THE REWARD OF ENTERPRISE

As his share of the National Income the owner of a business receives a reward that is known as *"profits"*. In practice, he calculates this share by deducting from his total receipts all payments he has to make to outside parties, *i.e.*, his total expenses, and the residue he regards as his profit—the reward or return that accrues to him for the part that he plays in industry.

NATURE

Now "profits" in the foregoing sense usually comprises several elements, additional to what the economist regards as *pure* profit. A fishmonger, for example, may manage and control his business, provide any capital that is necessary, perhaps employ several assistants, and himself work in the shop. Further, he may own the land on which his business premises are built, and he probably provides a "reserve fund" for maintenance and replacement charges in order to keep his shop and equipment in good order and up-to-date condition. Hence, out of the total reward that the fishmonger gets from his business, he expects a return for all his efforts and capital investment in the business, and also an annual allowance for the cost of keeping up or maintaining his premises and equipment.

When we analyse his reward, therefore, we see that it includes wages for his labour as a worker, wages of management for his efforts in controlling the business, interest on his capital, rent on his land, and depreciation and maintenance charges. The parts of his reward that represent the payments he receives for the services of his land, his labour, his capital and for his work as manager are true costs of production. If he did not provide these factors himself, he would have to pay other people for the use of them; so, in reckoning the return that he gets from the business, it is right that he should allow for payment for the use of the factors he himself supplies.

But few people would open shops and take the risk of starting and organising any form of business if they were not likely to make for themselves something more than mere wages for their labour, interest on their capital and rent for their land. There is, of course, much to be said for the independence of owning and running one's own business; but that in itself would not compensate a man for the risk, worry and trouble of getting a business started and keeping it on its feet.

The fact is that, over and above the return that the owner of a private business gets for the use of his land, his labour and his capital, he expects to get also a return —which is *profit—for giving birth to the idea, for setting the business in motion and for bearing the risk involved in the venture.*

This profit is a *residue* that may or may not emerge after all other factors of production, including those that may be supplied by the owner of the business himself, have been rewarded.

We can see the distinction between pure profit and the other forms of reward if we consider a new business in which all the other factors are provided *from outside sources*. In such a case, the entrepreneur rents the land, borrows all the capital he requires, and hires men to do the work. He himself organises the business and takes all the risk. He undertakes that the landowner will get his rent, that the hired labourers will receive their wages, and that the lender of capital will get the interest on his money. After paying all expenses the entrepreneur gets for himself anything that is left over. But the difference between his reward and the other rewards is that the latter are all *fixed beforehand by contract*; the rent is so much, the wages so much, and the interest on the capital so much. The only reward that is uncertain, that cannot be foretold until the business has run for a time, is the pure profit that belongs to the man who carries the risk of success or failure.

If the factors are not provided from outside sources, but are all supplied by the entrepreneur himself, as in the case of a one-man business, then he must make due allowance for the different rewards before he can ascertain his true or net profit. This is what he gets by conducting a business over and above what he could get by selling his labour elsewhere for wages, by hiring his land to someone else for rent and by lending his capital out at interest.

In any business, therefore, any elements in profits that constitute the return or reward to other factors are costs of production which must be deducted before net profit can be ascertained.

RISK-BEARING

There are certain risks in business and industry that can be passed on to others. Business men do not, usually, bear the direct risk of fire or of theft. These risks are carried by specialist institutions, insurance companies and underwriting firms, which, in return for the payment of an annual premium, relieve the business world of such burdens. But the risks borne by the entrepreneur himself are those that cannot be covered by insurance or any other form of specific contract. No insurance company will cover a gold-mining company against the possibility of its mine having very little gold in it, or the producer of a play against the failure of the play, or a business man against a rise in the price of raw materials, or against a change in fashion or a new invention that may ruin the demand for his products.

Most of the risk of business arises because *most production is carried on in anticipation of a demand that may not be realised*. A firm may design and produce a baby car within the financial reach of the masses, but as soon as it is put on the market, petrol-rationing may operate and scarcely a car may be sold. In the past much money was put into roller-skating rinks, but in the early days most of it was lost because the public was not enthusiastic. Owners of roadhouse bathing-pools take a big risk, because their takings are dependent on the weather, and in a bad summer they are likely to lose heavily.

Risks of this kind are true uncertainties; they cannot be insured against or contracted for in advance, and profit is the reward that the entrepreneur receives for assuming them. In so far as the entrepreneur, by the use of his knowledge and skill, can *reduce* risks inherent in his business, he receives a wage for mental labour of the highest type. But for his service in *assuming* risks that cannot be reduced by delegation or by any other device, his reward is profit.

The actual conditions of practical business show that this conception of profits is a close approximation to the truth. The entrepreneur or organiser of a large concern can determine fairly accurately in advance what rates he must pay for land, capital and labour for any given output which he may wish to achieve. But his rate of profit is always uncertain: it must reflect the result of his enterprise and his judgment. The services of land, capital and labour must be remunerated whether profits are made or not; their prices are pre-determined and regular, and are generally paid in cash before the results of the year's working have been or can be ascertained.

The bearing of risks is necessary for the progress of

society. Society would not have progressed very far if no one had been willing to bear the risks of undertaking new enterprise, *e.g.*, railways, the cinema, the wireless and television. Profit, therefore, may be regarded as Society's reward to those who successfully bear the risks inseparable from progress.

VARIATION IN PROFITS

Profits vary between different industries, because the risk varies from one industry to another. The greater the risk, the larger the reward that ultimately falls to those who have been bold enough to venture where others have feared to tread. The making of bread, for example, involves little risk, and the rate of profit of the baker is generally low. Where risks are great, as for instance in gold mining or oil production or rubber planting, there may be a heavy loss; but if profits are made, they are likely to be large.

The fact that profit may reach such munificent proportions in the case of producers of exceptional enterprise and of outstandingly good judgment is the mainspring of modern industry, and the force which impels entrepreneurs to great effort. Without this incentive to the business organiser, much land, labour and capital would remain idle, or at least be employed to much less advantage. The greater the efficiency of the various factors and of the industrial machine as a whole, the more the entrepreneur will benefit in the amount of his profit. But the greater efficiency of the industrial machine must unquestionably be an advantage to the community as a whole, and in this respect the interests of the entrepreneur and of the community coincide.

In view of the risks that are inseparable from business enterprise, it is to be expected that losses are frequently incurred. Firms may lose part of their capital, and business men may find that their total costs have not been covered by their receipts, so that the amount available as the reward for their services is less than they would have earned if they had worked for other people. On the whole, however, able entrepreneurs are scarce and the successful ones reap substantial rewards.

The Entrepreneur in Modern Industry

It is not always an easy matter to identify the entrepreneur in modern industry. In the days when the one-man business and the partnership predominated, he could easily be distinguished. When the person who controls a business is also the person who takes the risk, or when two or more persons in partnership share the control and also the risk, then clearly those persons are the entrepreneurs. To-day, however, the predominant form of industrial organisation is the public company, where control is in the hands of specialists and risk is borne by those who supply the capital in return for the prospect of sharing in the profits.

Company organisation involves the collection of savings from a large number of people and the transference of the capital so accumulated to those who are prepared to employ it in industry. Investors choose their own method and form of investment, and to that extent personally assume the risks of the business to which they entrust their savings. They may take up *debentures*, and so become entitled to interest, irrespective of profits and, if things go wrong, they have a first claim on the property of the concern; they may take *preference shares* which ensure for them a fixed rate of dividend payable as a first charge out of profits; or they may become *ordinary shareholders* entitled to the balance of profits.

These ordinary shareholders are the true risk-bearers in industrial organisation to-day. They delegate the control of the business to paid executives, but in fact assume the main risks of the business and their return cannot be settled *on any prearranged contractual basis*. The return to debenture-holders is a contractual one, fixed before the money is advanced and paid before profits are ascertained. The return to preference shareholders is also contractual in character, and though it may not be forthcoming if no profits are made, it is a fixed payment that must be met before the balance of profit is distributed. *The return to ordinary shareholders, however, is essentially of a residual nature*, depending on the success of the business. Their dividend may fluctuate widely from year to year, and their capital is the first to be treated as lost if the business does not succeed.

The essential function of the entrepreneur, the bearing of risks, is thus of a *passive* nature so far as the ordinary shareholder is concerned. The shareholder does not personally take part in the direction of the enterprise, but if it fails, he as the risk-bearer pays the penalty; he is the last in the chain of responsibility.

In a nationalised industry, the function of risk-bearing does not disappear. When the State assumes the rôle of entrepreneur, the risk falls on the Exchequer, and ultimately on the taxpayer.

CHAPTER XIII

INTERNATIONAL TRADE AND EXCHANGE

INTERNATIONAL TRADE or FOREIGN TRADE means the exchange of goods between the countries of the world. It is the result of the extension to the world as a whole of the principles of the division of labour and the localisation of industry that apply, as we have already noted, within the boundaries of a country. And just as these forms of organisation increase industrial efficiency, so does international trade add to the efficiency of each country and enhance the benefit it may derive from the enjoyment of the world's goods. England imports oranges from Spain because she cannot grow them herself, whilst Spain imports certain machinery from Britain because her industrial organisation is not suited for its manufacture.

The object of all international trade is, of course, the same as that which underlies all forms of exchange—to obtain the greatest possible advantage from the exchange of one kind of commodity for another—and there are no fundamental differences in principle between international trade and internal or domestic trade, *i.e.*, trade between different districts *of the same country*. All trade, whether within the boundaries of a country or not, arises from the same cause, *viz.*, specialisation and the consequent exchange of products between those who specialise.

ECONOMIC FRICTION IN INTERNATIONAL TRADE

The differences between home trade and international trade arise because the countries involved are entirely separate political units, each with its own language, laws, customs, currency, methods of trade and principles of business, all of which create barriers that prevent the free operation of economic forces. While, therefore, labour and capital move comparatively freely between different districts in the same country to those places that offer the best prospects of gain, both labour and capital move with difficulty between different countries. People are very reluctant to emigrate to a foreign land, even though they could earn higher wages there, and capitalists are chary of incurring the risks that attend investment in foreign enterprises.

Although the restrictions on mobility are largely due to the difficulties that arise in learning a new language and becoming acquainted with different laws, customs and monetary systems, they arise also from sentiment and attachment to one's native land, from fear of conditions in an unknown country, from poverty (making movement impossible) and ignorance of the advantages to be gained by living in another country.

Such factors are all more or less *passive*. There are, in addition, various *active* factors that operate to distinguish international trade from domestic trade. Governments often take active measures to prevent the free passage of goods and the movement of people into or away from their territories. They may impose duties on certain goods, or even prohibit altogether the entry of goods from certain countries. They may take action to restrict or to prohibit the movement of labour and capital by means of immigration regulations or by the control of capital exports, *e.g.*, they may prohibit foreign investments.

As a result of the operation of these factors, the fundamental principles underlying international trade are often obscured, and economists, therefore, treat the question of international trade differently from that of home trade.

The Advantages of Specialisation

International trade arises because of the advantages it brings to the countries that take part in it. It is clearly beneficial *when a country is able to import a commodity it could not possibly produce itself*. Britain, for example, cannot possibly grow rubber; the Congo has few facilities for manufacturing textile goods. Both Britain and the Congo, therefore, benefit by exchanging rubber for textiles.

Even if a country is physically able to produce the goods it usually imports, it is nevertheless worth while for that country to import them from another country which can *produce them more cheaply*. Britain, for instance, *might* conceivably grow grapes in hot-houses for making wine, instead of importing wine from France and other countries where grapes grow abundantly and cheaply. The cost of such production would, however, be enormous, because the climate of Britain is not suitable, and the appropriate growing conditions would have to be produced artificially. It is, therefore, better for Britain to apply her productive resources to goods that she can produce at a low cost, *e.g.*, woollens, and to use those woollens to pay for wine imported from France and other countries which have greater natural advantages for the cultivation of the vine. In this way, both France and Britain gain.

The Theory of Comparative Costs

But a lower cost of production is not sufficient in itself to explain all movements of goods from one country to another. Why, for example, should Britain—the finest dairy country in the world—rely on Denmark for butter and cheese? The answer is that it pays Britain better to concentrate on manufactures and to obtain butter from Denmark, because her superiority in manufactures is greater than her superiority in dairy farming, and she thereby gets a greater accession of wealth from every unit of labour and capital by employing that unit in manufacture rather than in dairying. Britain wants butter and Denmark wants machinery. Britain prefers to get the butter from Denmark rather than produce it herself, because she is thereby enabled to employ her labourers and her capital in occupations which make their use more profitable. For the same reason Denmark sells butter and buys machinery or clothes. In the long run both sides benefit by such an arrangement, and in both countries there is an economy of both capital and effort in obtaining the satisfaction of wants.

For example, Britain may, with the same outlay of labour and capital, produce ten times as much machinery or five times as much dairy produce as Denmark, which is thus at an absolute disadvantage in both sorts of production, *i.e.*, it *can* produce both, but only at a higher cost than Britain. It will thus be to their mutual advantage for Britain to concentrate on producing machinery, and Denmark to concentrate on dairying. Britain will exchange her machinery for the dairy produce of Denmark, and both countries will have cheaper machinery and dairy produce than if they tried to satisfy their wants independently. A simple example will demonstrate the truth of this position.

Suppose that with one unit of expenditure on machinery and one on dairy produce there is produced in:

	Machinery.	Dairy Produce.
Britain . . .	10 units	5 units
Denmark . . .	1 ,,	1 ,,
Total . . .	11 ,,	6 ,,

Two units of expenditure in each country, therefore, will produce 11 units of machinery and 6 units of dairy

produce. But if Britain concentrates her 2 units of outlay on machinery, and Denmark concentrates hers on
dairying, there will be produced in:

	Machinery.	Dairy Produce.
Britain . . .	20 units	
Denmark . . .		2 units
Total . . .	20 ,,	2 ,,

There is a gain of 9 units of machinery, but a loss of
4 units of dairy produce. Since, however, the expenditure required to produce 4 units of dairy produce will
produce only 8 units of machinery in England and 4
units of machinery in Denmark, it is clear that 9 units
of machinery are, in terms of productive effort, worth
more than 4 units of dairy produce in both countries.
Hence, when Britain specialises on machinery and Denmark on dairying, the productive powers of both countries are more efficiently employed. The resulting net
gain will be shared between the two countries, the actual
share of each depending on the relative value of machines
and dairy produce, which, in turn, will depend on the
relative bargaining strength of the countries. Clearly,
however, anything better than 5 units of dairy produce
for 10 units of machinery will benefit Britain, and anything better than 5 units of machinery for 5 units of
dairy produce will benefit Denmark. A rate of 7 units of
machinery for 5 units of dairy produce is possible and
would benefit both.

We see, then, that a country does not necessarily produce for export goods that it can produce at a lower
absolute cost (measured in expenditure of capital and
effort) than another country. It tends to export those
goods in the production of *which it has a greater relative
advantage, i.e.*, the goods in which its superiority is most

marked, or its inferiority least marked. Conversely, a country does not necessarily import goods because it can only produce them at a higher absolute cost than another country. A country imports those goods in the production of which its relative superiority is least, or its relative inferiority greatest.

This position is summed up as the *Law of Comparative Costs*, which states that a country will tend to concentrate on the production for export of those goods in which its superiority is most marked, or its inferiority least marked, and will import those things in which its superiority is least marked, or its inferiority most marked. More briefly, we can say that *a country tends to export those goods that it can produce with the greatest relative advantage*, i.e., *at the lowest comparative cost.*

Although this principle of comparative costs is applied mainly in connection with international trade, we can see it in operation in all forms of production. It is merely another way of stating that the advantages of the division of labour are gained, not by persons doing what they can do best, but *by persons doing what they can do relatively better than other people.* A bank manager may be better in dealing with customers than at managing the bank, but providing his superiority over his clerks is greater in managing the bank, it is better for him to manage the bank and for the tellers to remain at the counter. This principle of specialisation in the direction where the comparative advantages are greatest, or the comparative disadvantages are least, is responsible for the localisation of industries in districts of a country, and for localisation between countries.

COMPETITION IN INTERNATIONAL TRADE

In view of this theory, it may seem strange that countries should compete to sell their goods in world markets, when the world as a whole would gain if countries specialised in producing those goods for which their comparative advantages were greatest. This apparent contradiction between theory and practice can be explained (apart from the complications introduced by economic nationalism and tariffs—see below) by the fact that *it is only by the process of competition that countries can discover for what products they possess the greatest comparative advantages.*

The productive system of the world is not static; it is constantly changing. New sources of materials and new methods of production are continuously being discovered, and forces are continually operating to vary the advantages of a country for the production of certain goods. A country may thus lose the comparative advantage she once had in the production of, say, textiles, and be forced to cede pride of place to another country in which more favourable conditions have arisen. A second reason is that because of the operation of the Law of Diminishing Returns, a country may find it profitable to grow only part of the produce required. The whole supply could be obtained at home only at a much higher cost, so part of it is imported from abroad. For these reasons, *international trade must remain competitive although it is fundamentally complementary.* Competition will reveal that a country is not so well suited for the production of a certain commodity, relative to other countries, as she was in the past.

THE TERMS OF TRADE

A country exchanges its exports for imports. At any moment, there is a relationship between the total physical amount of exports from a country and the total physical amount of imports to it from all countries. This relationship is expressed as the terms of trade, *i.e.*, the amount of exports that have to be given for a certain amount of imports.

From time to time, the terms of trade change. Because of price changes, exports and imports may cost more or less and a country might have to sell more or less goods in order to obtain a given amount of imports. If the demand for a particular import, the price of which has risen, is inelastic, *e.g.*, wheat into Britain, then the importing country will have to sell more exports to pay for a given amount of imports. If the demand for the imports is elastic, less will be imported.

When a country receives a greater volume of imports for a given amount of exports, the terms of trade are favourable and they are unfavourable if she has to sell more goods for a given volume of imports. These movements in the terms of trade affect the balance of payments of a country.

THE BALANCE OF PAYMENTS

Goods passing from one country to another have to be paid for, and international trade involves the creation of debts between countries. Over a given period—say, a year—a country owes sums to various countries for goods she has imported from them, but sums are also owing to her for goods she has exported to other countries. When the total sums owing to a country exceed the total sums owing by her, she is said to have a *Favourable Balance of Trade*, *i.e.*, a surplus on international account; when the total amount due by a country exceeds the amount due to her, she has an *Adverse Balance of Trade*, *i.e.*, a deficit on international account.

Payments for commodities are not, however, the only items entering into international indebtedness. Debts arise between countries for other reasons, as, for example, for shipping, insurance and financial services, and in respect of war debts, expenses of tourists and remittances to nationals residing abroad. Though much reduced in consequence of the Second World War, the payments to

Britain by the countries of the world on account of
freights, insurance, commissions and interest on loans,
amount to millions annually. If, for instance, Britain
does insurance and banking business for Denmark, the
premiums and commissions are payments due from
Denmark to Britain. Again, when Britain lent money to
the Argentine, the yearly interest on the debt was a
payment due from the Argentine to Britain. Conversely, Britain owes money to countries which perform
services for her.

A service performed by one country for another is
known as an *"invisible export"* of the country performing
it, because a payment is due for that service just as if
something tangible had been exported. Similarly, services received by a country, for which it has to pay, are
"invisible imports" into that country.

To find the state of indebtedness of a country with
respect to the world as a whole, *i.e.*, her balance of payments, we must compare her total exports (visible and
invisible) with her total imports (visible and invisible).
In the long run, a country's payments for imports and
her receipts for exports must balance.

A country which has a surplus on her balance of payments may receive the balance in gold; or may lend the
debtor countries sufficient to wipe out the balance and
receive interest on the loan; or may leave the money
owing to her in the debtor country and use it when
required to purchase goods or to pay for services or to
lend to a third country. The country which has a deficit
on her balance of payments will thus have to lose gold,
or borrow the amount of the balance from other countries,
or hold money at the disposal of the creditor countries.

We can see, therefore, that if we consider visible and
invisible imports and exports, a country's total exports
must, in the long run, balance her total imports; *exports
must pay for imports*. It follows that if a country's ex-

ports fall, her imports will also fall unless the deficiency in exports can be made good in the ways specified above. We can now realise the importance to Britain of keeping up the volume of her exports.

In addition to the ways already indicated, international trade is further complicated because countries are not concerned solely with the advantages to be obtained from specialisation and the exchange of goods. *They seek to maintain equilibrium in the balance of payments,* or at least to keep the excess of imports as low as possible, because a continued net deficit of any extent involves serious disadvantages. A country may become heavily indebted to other countries if the unfavourable situation continues, and, ultimately, may find herself unable to obtain essential imports.

Small wonder, then, that countries watch most carefully their balance of payments with other countries and seek means to correct an adverse position should it arise. Generally, they do this by means of restrictions on the import of goods, since most of the items giving rise to international indebtedness are concerned with goods, coupled with various expedients designed to increase exports, *e.g.,* preferences to export industries in the way of finance and licences to import raw materials.

TARIFFS

An effective method of correcting an adverse balance of payments was, at one time, to restrict the import of goods by imposing on them duties, known as *tariffs*. Under a tariff system, the price of the imported goods rises by at least the amount of the tariff and importation is consequently checked. Tariffs are most commonly imposed on goods that the country can produce herself, but they may be used also to curtail the imports of goods that she cannot produce because she wishes to restrict their use, for example, drugs.

Tariffs may also be imposed for other reasons, *e.g.*, to foster the growth of "infant" industries that cannot develop in face of foreign competition, or to foster the growth of industries that may be vital to the national safety in time of war.

PROTECTION *versus* FREE TRADE

In an ideal world, there would be *Free Trade, i.e.*, a complete absence of duties on imports, and all countries would reap to the full the advantage of international territorial specialisation, just as different parts of Britain benefit from the productive advantages of all the other parts.

There has, however, always been a strong tendency for nations to impose tariffs on imports for the purpose of protecting home industries from the competition of foreign goods.[1] Many reasons have been put forward in support of *Protection*, now generally applied by all the trading countries of the world, including Britain, which for many years was the traditional home of Free Trade.

Protectionists argue that a policy of general protection is bound to benefit the country as a whole. Free Traders admit that *any given industry* may benefit by a tariff because the supply of its goods on the market is reduced, but they maintain that the *country as a whole* will not benefit if all industries are protected. Export industries in particular will suffer, because if a country will not buy foreign goods, foreigners will be unable to buy her goods.

Protectionists argue that protective duties ensure that there will be a variety of industries within the country. As a result of Free Trade a country might concentrate on one or two industries and rely on other countries to

[1] An import duty on goods not produced at home, or on goods that are produced at home but on which an equivalent excise duty is levied, is not a *protective* duty, but a *revenue* duty.

supply many needs. Such a position, it is claimed, may lead to disaster if supplies of vital goods from abroad are cut off (*e.g.*, during war time) and if the demand for the products of the particular country falls away, or if the relative advantages for these industries decline. These dangers, say protectionists, can be avoided by establishing a variety of industries, even though some are inefficient and have to be protected by tariffs on competing imports. On the other hand, it is doubtful whether the existence of the danger here contemplated can be proved in the present highly diversified condition of international trading and the many alternative sources of supply of most important products.

Protection is also claimed to be necessary if a nation is to be independent of foreign sources of supply of vital commodities (especially food) during times of war. It is argued that, if a country allows its agricultural industry to decline because of the competition of foreign foodstuffs, and because it apparently pays the people to specialise on manufactures, the country is likely to be hard hit in time of war when foreign food supplies are cut off or curtailed.

Two world wars have served to give point to this argument, but much of its validity obviously depends on the extent to which specialisation is allowed to go. In Britain, wartime blockade led to maximum efforts being made to stimulate agricultural production. There followed the post-war necessity for keeping imports to a minimum, so that it was no longer a case of choosing between protecting agriculture or relying on cheaper products imported from abroad. In any event, it is extremely doubtful whether any measure of protection would enable Britain to become agriculturally self-supporting.

Another argument for Protection is that it is necessary to prevent the *dumping* into a country of foreign goods made by low-wage labour. To this argument the Free

Trader had no effective answer, but he points to the benefits of cheap imports to the consumer, to the difficulty of determining what is low-wage labour in view of the great differences in standards of living between different countries, and to the facts that low-wage labour is usually inefficient labour and that labour costs in such conditions are generally high.

THE INFANT INDUSTRY ARGUMENT

There is perhaps more justification for a tariff where an "infant industry" is concerned. An *infant industry* is one newly started, or about to be started, in any particular country, as was the motor-car industry when it was first started in Britain, years after it had attained vast dimensions in the United States.

The argument of Protectionists is that the weak infant industry, lacking at first the advantages of old-established industries in foreign countries, cannot quickly develop to the point where the natural advantages of the country will enable it to meet successfully the competition of well-established foreign industries. Hence, if no steps are taken to protect it, it may never come into being or, once started, it will decay and die. If it is protected by a tariff on foreign imports of products similar to its own, however, it can grow behind the shelter of the tariff, and ultimately become so strong that it can stand on its own feet, when the tariff can be discontinued.

The arguments are valid in theory, but in practice infant industries never seem to "grow up". Instead, vested interests are created around them, and any suggestions for the removal of the duty are strenuously resisted on the ground that the industry is not yet strong enough. The practical result is that even when the industry is fully developed, the prices of its products are kept higher than they need be because of the monopoly conferred on home producers by the tariff.

For these reasons, Free Traders are willing to approve a protective duty to assist an infant industry, only when two conditions necessary for the protection of the home consumer are fulfilled: (*a*) the industry must be really suitable for the country, otherwise it can never succeed; (*b*) the duty must be removed, in spite of protests, after a specified period during which, having regard to all circumstances, the industry should have reached maturity.

The desire for freer international trade in the postwar period found expression in the International Trade Organisation (I.T.O.). The most significant work of this Organisation was an international agreement, the General Agreement on Tariffs and Trade (G.A.T.T.), which came into operation in 1948. A wide range of tariff reductions was made in member countries, but as the machinery works slowly other measures were devised to promote international trade, notably the E.C.M.

THE EUROPEAN COMMON MARKET

This Market was set up in 1958 by France, West Germany, Italy, Belgium, Holland and Luxembourg (the last three constituting the *Benelux* countries) which were already members of the European Economic Community, with the purpose of abolishing *internal* tariffs on goods passing between the member countries and establishing a common *external* tariff for all members as against all countries outside the Market. The Market is really a *customs union*; it gradually reduced import duties and trade restrictions between the members until all restrictions were abolished and the Market is now a free trade area. Britain did not enter the Market as an original member because of her agricultural position and her Commonwealth obligations; she formed instead a *European Free Trade Area* (E.F.T.A.), with Sweden, Norway, Denmark, Switzerland, Austria and Portugal. In this Area, tariffs between member countries have been gradually eliminated but each country arranges its own policy with regard to external tariffs.

The European Common Market prospered and it appeared that this organisation would assist in the expansion of world trade so urgently needed. Britain required wider markets in which to sell the products of her expanding industrial units and, with the other members of E.F.T.A., applied for membership, but it was not until 1972 that her application was successful.

THE FOREIGN EXCHANGES

One of the complications in international trade is the existence of different monetary systems in different countries. A British pound note is legal tender in Britain, but not in France, where the legal tender money consists of franc notes and coin. If an Englishman has to pay a debt in francs, as, for example, for goods imported from France, he must buy the necessary number of francs through his banker from the Foreign Exchange Market, where many kinds of currencies are dealt in. He will pay, say, £1 for 13·30 francs and this will be the *rate of exchange* between francs and pounds. The *rate of exchange* is thus *the price at which the currency of one country is expressed in terms of the currency of another country*.

In Britain from 1939 to 1951, the Bank of England controlled all foreign exchange dealings and fixed most exchange rates. In December, 1951, the London Foreign Exchange Market was re-opened and its members became free to quote their own rates. The official parity for the dollar (to take an example) remained at $2·40, but the Bank would intervene, to buy or sell in such a way as to bring back the market rate to within one per cent of parity, only if the market rate went outside the limits of $2·37¼ and $2·42¾. In 1971 the dollar was devalued and its rate with £1 sterling fell to 2·59 3/16.

If artificial controls do not operate, the price of francs in terms of sterling is determined fundamentally in the same way as other prices, *i.e.*, by the relation of demand and supply. *The demand* for francs in London comes from those who wish to obtain rights to francs available for use in France, to pay for goods bought from France or for services performed for them in France, or perhaps to send to a relative in France. Such people want to exchange sterling for francs. *The supply* of francs in London comes from those who wish to sell for sterling certain rights to francs that they possess. These persons may have sold goods to France or have performed services for Frenchman, and so become entitled to francs in payment. They wish to exchange these francs for their own currency, sterling.

Thus, foreign exchange is concerned with the sale and purchase of rights to currencies available as purchasing power in other countries. A man going to France for a holiday must have rights to francs there, and, subject to compliance with any exchange-control regulations that may exist, his banker obtains francs for him. In practice, supplies and demands are correlated by banks and foreign exchange dealers, who quote rates for buying and selling specified currencies. These rates fluctuate from day to day, in accordance with conditions of supply and demand on the market.

If many people in London want francs, and francs are in short supply, the price of francs in terms of sterling will tend to rise, *i.e.*, the rate of exchange will move in favour of francs and against sterling. If, on the other hand, there are many sellers of francs for sterling, and few buyers, the price of francs in terms of sterling will tend to fall, *i.e.*, the rate of exchange will move against francs and for sterling.

We can now see another reason why countries wish to avoid a deficit on their balance of payments. A country with a deficit owes more than it is owed. Its demand for foreign currencies is consequently greater than the demands of other countries for its currency. The result is a fall in the external value of its currency. It has to pay more for foreign currencies, and finds it dearer to buy goods abroad. If the fall in the value of the country's currency were allowed to continue, the deficit might be ultimately wiped out, but this process is not viewed with pleasure, largely because a constantly unfavourable rate of exchange lowers a country's prestige and raises the cost of its imports. Then tariffs and, more particularly, import restrictions and "export-drives", are used to control the balance of payments and to prevent or reduce a deficit.

Since 1939—and in many cases much earlier—most States have continuously exerted official influence on rates, mainly by (1) the establishment of *Exchange Equalisation Funds* (designed to provide a reservoir of foreign-exchange available for smoothing out variations in rates)—thus, by intervening in the market, buying or selling as occasion requires, the Bank of England, using the resources of the British Exchange Equalisation Account, can bring about a rise or fall in the market rates; (2) stimulating the external demand for the national currency by pursuing economic and fiscal policies designed to increase the country's exports; and (3) by limiting the domestic demand for foreign currencies by restricting or prohibiting imports of certain commodities and regulating the transfer of funds abroad.

Thus, although dealers in the Foreign Exchange Market have a measure of freedom to fix rates on the basis of the prevailing supply and demand, the actual supply and demand are very largely determined by the government's exchange-control policy at the moment. Moreover, the regulations of the International Monetary Fund, to which most trading States belong, bind member-nations to take steps to ensure that the "spot" rate of exchange (*i.e.*, for immediate delivery of currency) does not deviate by more than one per cent. from the declared parity.

In consequence, exchange rates fluctuate less than when supply and demand were not subject to the same degree of official control and most currencies were freely convertible.

The Purchasing-Power-Parity Theory

While *in the short run* the rate of exchange between two currencies fluctuates according to supply and demand, *in the long run* the rate will tend to rest at a level that *reflects the relative purchasing powers of the currencies in terms of goods and services.*

For instance, if a certain collection of goods costs £100 in Britain and 1,330 francs in France at any particular time, then the purchasing-power parity between francs and sterling in terms of those goods is £1 = 13·30 francs, and the market rate of exchange between francs and pounds will tend to move to that level. If the actual rate in the market is, say, 13·31 francs to the £, it will pay British importers to change their pounds into francs, buy goods in France and sell them in Britain. (We are omitting transport costs, import restrictions, and tariffs for simplicity.) The consequent increase in the London demand for francs, and the decrease in the French demand for sterling, will tend to move the rate to £1 = 13·30 francs. The converse is true if the rate is, say, 13·29 francs to the £.

Although many qualifications are necessary to this broad statement of the theory, it is undoubtedly a clue to exchange movements over a long period, when exchange rates move in accordance with the purchasing powers of the currencies concerned, *i.e.*, in accordance with changes in price levels.

The operation of the theory is, however, greatly impeded, and often obscured, by exchange transactions that have nothing to do with the relative price levels in the countries concerned. Other influences are speculation in currencies, the flow of funds between countries for investment purposes, the operations of Governments designed to regulate the rate of exchange for their currencies.

CHAPTER XIV

THE STATE AND ITS FUNCTIONS

WE have been concerned in the foregoing pages with an
economic structure of Society that is based on private
initiative and private enterprise, and which, by reason
of the forces of competition and of self-interest, is largely
self-regulating. It has been assumed in our study that
law and order are maintained in the community by some
controlling authority that protects men from violence
and robbery, ensures that they carry out their contracts
with their fellows, and guards them against destitution.
This controlling authority is the *State*, and, in the modern
economic community, the State, working through Parliament or other ruling authority, performs many important functions.

STATE ACTIVITY

Originally, the only functions of a State were to protect
its citizens from *external* attacks by the citizens of other
States and to maintain *internal* order. Gradually, these
functions took on a wider meaning. To maintain order,
an elaborate system of police and justice had to be built
up, highways had to be controlled and maintained,
methods of communication had to be developed, the
powers of the rich and powerful had to be carefully regu-
lated, and the poor had to be protected against oppres-
sion.

From the mere protection of property and persons, the
functions of the State were extended to embrace various
measures for controlling trade and business relationships
and for combating the evils of poverty and disease. The
State undertook the provision of social services, such as

free education, free medical services, housing subsidies and assistance for the unemployed, and in a modern community it now performs an increasing variety of controlling and other functions which substantially influence the daily life of its citizens.

The social services of general utility to the community that are undertaken by the State cannot be left to private enterprise either because of their magnitude or because of the absence of monetary reward. Few individuals can be expected to have sufficient solicitude for the general good of the citizens of their town as to furnish them with parks and playing-fields, or with schools for their children, or with well-paved streets and good roads for the conduct of their social and business activities. The value of such services is immeasurable, and by contributing to the health, welfare and efficiency of the people, they materially affect the productivity of the community as a whole.

In the provision of such public services it is now generally agreed that State intervention is necessary, although some controversy exists as to the extent to which it should proceed. Some think that the modern State does far too much in this direction, whereas others are equally convinced that it could do a great deal more to help its citizens to a fuller and better life.

Even more controversial is the extent to which the State should directly interfere with and take part in the business of the community. Should the State interfere with the free flow of goods between its own people and those of other countries, as by the imposition of restrictive tariffs and exchange-control or by the payment of subsidies or of bounties on exports? Is the control of the railway system, of the mines and, indeed, of industry generally, a reasonable and proper function of modern government? How far is government interference justified as between employer and employed, or as between consumer and monopolistic producer? To what extent should the elected representatives of a people interfere to regulate the productive activities of that people, and intervene to arrange a different distribution of wealth

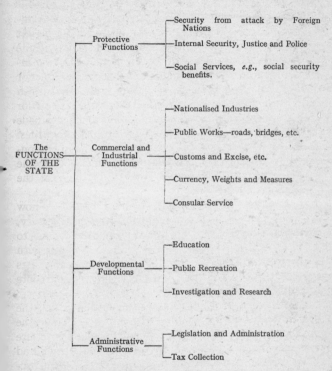

from that which results from the play of such economic forces as have been already discussed in this book?

State control over many aspects of economic life became essential in war, and paved the way for increasing government intervention in industry and commerce. In Britain, impetus was given to this trend by the election in 1945 of a government pledged to carry out a comprehensive programme of nationalisation. In consequence of the nationalisation of such industries as coal-mining, railways and inland transport, overseas communications, gas and electricity distribution, the functions of the State were extended to cover activities previously regarded as essentially those of private and/or municipal enterprise.

THE FUNCTIONS OF THE STATE

It is clearly the duty of the State to provide those goods and services that private enterprise *cannot be expected to provide*, especially protection against attack by foreign nations, involving the maintenance of an army, navy and air force, the organisation of civil defence and the operation of the secret service. Equally important is the maintenance of internal security involving the upkeep of the police force and of the judiciary system.

The State must also undertake, or at any rate promote, the provision of certain important commercial services and facilities that private enterprise is *not likely or fitted to provide*, as, for example, the construction and maintenance of roads, bridges, canals, riverways, harbours and lighthouses; the maintenance of the currency, including the minting and issue of coins; the institution and control of an effective system of weights and measures; and the organisation of a consular service for facilitating trade with other nations.

Then there are services which private enterprise *could not provide adequately*, but which are necessary for the best interests of the community, such as free education, both elementary and higher; the establishment and maintenance of museums and art galleries; the establishment and maintenance of hospitals; and the granting of funds or endowments for various other public welfare purposes. The State also provides, chiefly through local authorities, public recreation facilities, public baths, parks and lecture halls; undertakes scientific investigation and research, *e.g.*, for defence purposes and in connection with the improvement of crops, forestry and stock-breeding.

Most important of all is the assumption by the State of responsibility for its citizens when they are temporarily or permanently unable to keep their places as wage-earners in the economic system. In this direction the State provides relief to the poor, unfortunate and sick, so raising the national standard of health and morality, and helps those who, either from natural or acquired defects, are unable to hold their own in the struggle for existence.

THE INCOME OF THE STATE

The performance of the wide variety of non-trading functions involves very heavy annual expenditure. Every year modern States have to expend large sums on defence and civil service; for stores and materials of all kinds; in making grants for social services; in paying pensions and interest on loans incurred for exceptional expenditure that cannot be met out of the State income or revenue.

The State tries, but seldom succeeds nowadays, to pay its way without borrowing. It tries to keep its expenditure within the limits of its income, most of which is obtained by *taxation* of the people living within its boundaries.

TAXATION

A tax is a compulsory charge imposed by the State or public authority in respect of which no specific service *to the individual* is rendered in return. Taxes are not imposed as penalties for offences against the law, and

they are to be distinguished from the revenue received
by the State from any business it may carry on or from
specific services that it might perform for the individual.
Thus, the revenue received by the British Government
from the Post Office is not part of its income from taxation even though the Post Office charges are intended to

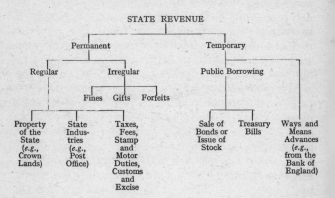

yield an annual surplus as a contribution towards State
revenue; it is composed of payments received for services
rendered by the Government to individuals; it represents
the proceeds of *prices* charged to the public for postal
services. There is a marked difference, for instance, between 25p charged to me for a telegram and 25p that
I pay as entertainment tax on entering a cinema. For the
former payment I get a valuable service; for the latter I
get nothing *direct* in return—it is just a tax, a means of
obtaining revenue for State purposes.

Taxes differ considerably in the burden they impose on
members of the community, in the facility with which
they can be collected, and in the net return that they
bring into the coffers of the State. Some taxes are
"bad" because they cause much hardship, or great in-

convenience, or involve considerable expense and trouble in collection, yielding only a small net return to the State.

ATTRIBUTES OF "GOOD" TAXES

A "good" tax must conform with certain recognised principles or *canons*. First, it must be *equitable*; the sacrifice involved must fall as equally as possible on rich and poor. This does not mean that rich and poor should pay the same amount of money or the same proportion of tax in relation to their income. A tax of £1 would mean little or nothing to a rich man, but would be a real burden to a poor man; a tax of 5p in the £ would be a greater burden to a poor man who had to pay £5 on £100 income, than it would be to a rich man who had to pay £50 on his £1000 income. The sacrifice represented by a payment of £5 by a poor man will usually be greater than that represented by a payment of £50 by a rich man. A fair tax system, consequently, should take less *proportionally* from the poor man than from the rich man.

Another important attribute required of a good tax is that it shall be *certain*—everyone must know what he has to pay, and the State must know what it has to receive. It would be most annoying to the individual, and detrimental to business, if a tax was indefinite and provision could not be made at the proper time to meet the tax payment because of uncertainty as to what it might be.

Good taxes are also *convenient*; they are levied at a time most convenient to the taxpayer, and they should also be *economical*—the less it costs to collect a tax, the better it is from the point of view of the State and of the individual as a member of the State.

A tax should also produce sufficient revenue to justify its imposition. Hence, one large tax which is known to be *productive* is preferable to several small taxes which are inconvenient or annoying to the taxpayer, and which involve much time and expense in collecting. It is an advantage, too, if it is possible to increase the rate of a tax without harmful effects in order to meet sudden or exceptional demands for revenue.

DIRECT AND INDIRECT TAXES

In this country, equity in taxation is achieved by using a combined system of taxation involving what are known as *direct* taxes and *indirect* taxes. A *direct tax* falls directly on the person who is intended to pay, as for example the income tax, the motor-car tax, dog and wireless licences and stamp duties. Of these the most important are the income tax, which in this country is imposed on all incomes after deducting specified allowances, surtax and death duties.

Indirect taxes, generally in the form of customs and excise duties, comprise duties on tea, sugar, tobacco and other commodities. They are paid in the first instance by importers and manufacturers, and are passed on to the consumer in the prices charged for the goods. In this way, even the poorest people who are exempt from most direct taxes, and in particular from the income tax, are made to contribute something towards the national revenue.

Another important indirect tax is *Purchase Tax*, payable on the wholesale price of a wide range of goods and collected eventually from the final customer. It is graduated and the rate varies with the nature of the commodity; it is not charged on essentials but is high on luxury articles.

INCOME TAX

The most important tax in the British fiscal system is the Income Tax, which is levied on all incomes above a certain exempted minimum, subject to certain allowances to avoid hardship in particular cases. Thus relief from a certain amount of tax is granted to married men in respect of their wives, while allowances are made to persons who have to support children or dependants. Earned income below certain maxima is taxed less heavily than unearned income, and the rate of the tax per £ increases as the total income increases, because people with higher incomes can usually afford to pay more than proportionately.

The tax has proved an essential financial instrument. It can be easily raised or lowered to meet the needs of the Exchequer. It conforms closely to the ideal of all taxation that persons should contribute to the coffers of the State in proportion to their ability to pay, for the income of an individual is the best single criterion of such ability. Also, the tax is borne by the person who is intended to bear it, and it cannot be "shifted" easily on to another person.

The tax on income has certain disadvantages, however. It does not make *full* allowance for the circumstances of particular individuals. When commodities such as tea and sugar are taxed, the individual who buys these articles buys only what he needs, so the tax that he pays in the price of the articles is related to his ability to pay. Income tax, however, must be paid by everyone according to the fixed scale, with certain allowances, *e.g.*, for dependants, but there are no allowances for such circumstances as permanent physical disability or ill health, which may render a given amount of income of less value to one individual than the same amount would be to another. Another objection to the income tax is that it is possible to evade the tax by making false returns, or to avoid the tax by resorting to various devices to circumvent the law.

To some extent evasion was made more difficult by the introduction of P.A.Y.E, pay-as-you-earn.

SUR-TAX

Sur-tax provides for the taxation of all income above a certain figure at a rate higher than the standard rate. The principle underlying this form of taxation is that of the diminishing utility of incomes over a certain figure, and its object is to secure a more equitable contribution to taxation from those who are the more fortunately situated. The general objections to high rates of income tax apply here also.

TAXATION AND PRODUCTION

The volume of production in a community depends on the amount of work done and on the amount of saving that has taken place. Production requires labour and capital, and the more there is of each, the greater will be the volume of production.

A good tax system should not harm the productive process, though it should operate to reduce the inequality of incomes. It may be that these two aims are mutually inconsistent, but this cannot be proved.

The ability to work and save will greatly influence the volume of production. Taxation that reduces the worker's ability to work will be harmful to production. Small incomes and necessaries of life should, therefore, be exempt. The exact demarcation of the exemption limit is a matter of difficulty, but the principle is sound, the limit depending on the cost of living necessary for efficiency.

Ability to save depends on the margin left after necessary expenses are met. Any taxation which is paid out of what would otherwise be saved does in fact reduce savings. Clearly, the larger part of savings is done by the rich, since they have a large margin. Taxation of the rich will, therefore, reduce savings, although the fact that certain people save less may not necessarily reduce the ability to save of the community as a whole. Redistributive taxation by the State may provide increased employment and higher incomes, so that more may be saved than before. When the State spends productively the resources it gets from taxation, the accumulation of capital will not suffer as a result of the reduced ability-to-save of a certain class of the population.

But serious results may eventually ensue if taxation is so heavy that it denudes industry of essential working capital and financial resources required for the replacement or extension of plant and equipment.

It is very difficult to estimate the effect of taxation on different persons as regards their desire to work and save. Some people who are taxed will work harder in order to maintain their net income; others will not think the extra effort worth while and may work less hard. Even if people do desire to alter the amount of work done, they cannot always do so, because most workers are under contractual engagements as regards hours. Heavy taxation may however make overtime rates unattractive. It is possible that the independent entrepreneur may consider that some project is not worth while undertaking because his profits will be highly taxed. The effect of taxation on willingness to work and save thus depends on the individual nature and the individual outlook, so that very little can be said except that very heavy rates of taxation will probably check production in some way. Although business men firmly believe something of the kind happens, it is difficult to discover actual cases.

While business men are prone to exaggerate the effects of a high income tax upon industry, it cannot be denied that a high tax does have adverse psychological effects on enterprise, and that reductions in the rates of tax tend to be followed by beneficial effects on industry because of the greater confidence created.

Those who oppose a high income tax sometimes argue that the tax is passed on to the consumer in the form of higher prices, with the result that demand is reduced and trade adversely affected. This argument is unsound, however. Price, as we have seen, is determined by supply and demand, and profit is made *after* the product is produced, so that a tax on that profit cannot influence the prices of goods that have already been sold. Moreover, income tax hits all incomes, regardless of the branch of production in which the incomes are made. There is, therefore, no inducement to transfer labour or any other factor of production from one employment (which would restrict the supply and raise the price of the product) for the factor would have to pay the same tax wherever it was employed.

Income tax does, however, represent an appropriation of part of a person's purchasing power, and for this reason he may reduce either his purchases or his savings, with consequent adverse effects on industry in either case. A further point is that all the profits of a business are subjected to income tax, *including that portion which is placed aside as a reserve for contingencies or as a means of further strengthening the business*, and in so far as these amounts are reduced by income tax, industry suffers.

GOVERNMENT BORROWING

Modern States, when faced with exceptional social service programmes or with enormous defence expenditure, cannot possibly meet all their expenses from the proceeds of taxation. Any Government that sought to do so would have to impose such a high rate of tax in order to bring in the necessary funds that would create discontent among the people, check production and risk internal revolt. Most Governments which are faced with exceptional expenditure, therefore, resort to borrowing and in a period of rising prices this is likely to be of advantage to the Government. The money interest that has to be paid on such loans is fixed and the payments made to the lenders represent a smaller proportion of the National Income than they did when the debt was incurred.

A sound principle adopted by modern Governments is that regular and recurring expenditure should be met out of taxation, but that *extraordinary* expenditure, such as the financing of development, nationalisation or emergency defence programmes, should be financed by short-period borrowing or long-period loans.

A short-term loan, as its name implies, is one that is repayable within a short time, *e.g.*, three months; a long-term loan is repayable only after a lapse of years.

In deciding which of these two forms to adopt, the Government must be guided by the situation at the moment. Temporary loans (sometimes called *unfunded debt*) are best when rates of interest are high, for the State would be unwise to enter into long-term obligations (*funded* debt) at high rates when there is a possibility of a fall in the rate. When rates are low, the opportunity can be taken to issue long-dated loans for the purpose of repaying floating debt incurred at higher rates of interest. There is usually no difficulty in issuing long-dated loans in times of low interest rates, for investors cannot find other outlets for their money, and a Government loan offers a long, secure investment.

It is a sound principle that a nation's unfunded debt should not be too large in proportion to the funded debt. The great evil of floating or unfunded debt is that it is likely to get out of hand; the Government responsible may too easily draw on the available resources of the money market and find itself saddled with a large debt that is repayable in a very short time. Moreover, if the available supplies of short-term funds are absorbed by Government borrowing, the operations of the money market are severely handicapped, while at the same time the Government deprives itself of a source from which it can readily obtain funds in emergency.

THE BURDEN OF GOVERNMENT LOANS

To understand the burden imposed upon a nation by the existence of a large *National Debt*, as the total public indebtedness is called, a distinction must be drawn between loans made to a State *by foreigners* and loans made *by its own citizens*.

Where the loan is an *external* one, then the borrowing Government has to pay people outside its boundaries not only interest on the loan, but also the principal when the loan is repaid, and the people so paid, *i.e.*, the creditors, can use the money to obtain goods and services from the borrowing country. If the borrowing country has used the borrowed money to create more *productive* goods (say, railways), then it will ultimately gain. Otherwise an external loan leads to a net burden, as will clearly be the case where the loan is used for *unproductive* purposes, *e.g.*, to finance a war or internal revolution.

The position is different where a Government borrows *from its own citizens*, for the payments it makes to the bondholders merely result in a rearrangement of income within the country. Money is received from taxpayers and transferred to bondholders, possibly the same people but more often from one group to another; for instance, from people actively working to those who have retired.

It cannot, however, be said that an internal debt for unproductive purposes, *e.g.*, a war, leads to no harmful effects. For one thing, the resources that were used in producing armaments could have been used in building houses, bridges, hospitals and so on, in which case both the present and future generations lose benefits they might have received. Secondly, a Government that has to meet heavy interest payments out of the annual tax receipts may be unable to raise taxation to a level necessary to meet the interest charge and might have to fall back on a curtailment of its expenditure, probably on social services, with ultimate disadvantages to the community as a whole, but more especially to the working classes.

The Government of Britain has now become a habitual borrower on a very extensive scale and the cost of servicing the debt is an important item in national expenditure. The higher the cost, the greater is the burden on the Exchequer which has to make provision for meeting the payments in the Budget presented every year to Parliament.

LOCAL AUTHORITIES

Apart from the functions discharged by the *central* Government, local authorities also perform important functions and require considerable revenue to meet their expenses. The bulk of this revenue comes from *local taxation*, which takes the form of *rates* levied by local authorities on the occupiers of buildings and land at so much in the £ on their value. Such property is assessed at a *rateable value*, based on the annual rent the property might be expected to yield, less certain annual charges, such as insurance and repairs.

The services received by people who pay rates are more easily identifiable than are the services received in return for the payment of national taxes. Rates are used largely for improving the amenities *of the locality* in which the rates are paid—for supplying street lighting, sanitation, roads, bridges and water. Hence, it is maintained that the *size* of the property on which rates are imposed is a fair indication of the benefits received, and that rates should therefore be *in proportion to* the value of the property taxed. Further, since the value of occupied property may be taken to vary with the means of the occupier, rates levied according to that value are regarded as a measure of the occupier's ability to pay.

It is not difficult, however, to suggest cases where the value of the property bears little relation to the income of the occupier. The occupier may have a relatively small income, but may find it necessary to maintain a large house because his family is large, or, as in the case of a doctor, because his professional dignity demands a large house. A man with a large income may choose to occupy a small house and spend his surplus income on other things—a car, for instance. In the case of business premises, too, the nature of the business carried on may lead to a lack of correspondence between the income received and the size of premises necessary to earn that income. A jeweller needs only a small shop to house his wares; a timber merchant needs considerable space for his business. The timber merchant will be more heavily rated than the jeweller, though the jeweller may receive a much higher income.

In view of such inequalities arising out of the fact that the value of the rated premises bears little relation to the income of the occupier, local taxation cannot be considered as conforming with the rule of ability to pay, except in a very general way. On the other hand, it meets the canons of convenience and economy; rates are easily levied and are usually collected with little difficulty.

VALUE ADDED TAX (V.A.T.)

This is an indirect tax similar to a tax on turnover or a sales tax. It is levied on final consumers in respect of most transactions, including the purchase of services and goods, e.g., hotel bills, motor cars, and road, rail and air fares, with concessions in the case of some necessaries. The tax is collected in instalments at each stage in the chain of production and assessed on the value added to the product by each process. In this the tax differs from the system of adding tax only when the product is sold. The tax paid by the final consumer is assessed on the price of the sale made to him minus the amount that has already been paid in the course of production. V.A.T. is a simplified system and its adoption is compulsory on all members of the European Common Market. Britain in preparation for her entry into the Market abolished certain taxes, *e.g.*, Corporation Tax and Selective Employment Tax.

TEST EXERCISES

Every reader should be able to deal successfully with the following exercises.

CHAPTER I

1. What is the chief characteristic of an economic problem?

2. How can an economist assist a Government or an individual to decide whether a proposed course of conduct is justifiable or not?

3. Examine the contention that private property is justified because its existence increases national wealth and productive efficiency.

4. How would you explain to a friend the benefit you hope to obtain from studying Economics?

5. What do you understand by the system of private enterprise? In such a system can there be State ownership and control of economic undertakings?

CHAPTER II

1. What do you understand by marginal utility? What is the practical importance of the theory?

2. What do you understand by elasticity of demand?

3. What two important principles regulate an individual's distribution of his expenditure in the various lines open to him?

4. Explain utility and discuss it from the economic standpoint. How can the utility of a thing be affected by (a) transport, and (b) time?

5. "Wants may be said to control production." How far do you agree with this statement?

CHAPTER III

1. What do you understand by capital? Do you regard the following as capital: (a) the River Thames; (b) the deeds of a house; (c) a house; (d) a surgeon's skill; (e) a surgeon's motor-car?

2. What is the difference between "productive" and "unproductive" labour? In what class would you place the following: (a) a porter in a railway station; (b) a cotton spinner; (c) a shop assistant; (d) an opera singer; (e) a soldier; (f) an amateur tennis player?

3. "Land is on a different footing from the other agents of production" (Marshall). What are the differences?

4. For what service does the entrepreneur receive his reward?

5. What do you understand by the Law of Diminishing Returns? How does it affect (a) the growing of foodstuffs; (b) the production of manufactures; (c) the production of minerals?

CHAPTER IV

1. What is meant by the division of labour? What are its effects on production and on the workers?

2. Why is the size of the typical business unit small in some industries and large in others?

3. What factors are responsible for the localisation of industries? Do you agree that the State should control the localisation of industries?

4. What do you understand by the Law of Increasing Returns?

5. What are the economies of scale? Are there any limits to the advantages of producing on a large scale?

CHAPTER V

1. Distinguish between variable and fixed costs. Show the importance of this distinction in relation to (a) railway rates and (b) the price of coal.

2. What do you understand by elasticity of supply? Why is supply elastic in some cases and not in others?

3. What does the business man mean by cost of production? In what circumstances, if at all, would he be prepared to sell below cost?

4. Do you agree that earthquakes and war are good for trade since employment is increased?

5. Discuss the relation between cost of production and price. Consider the case of (a) strawberries; (b) houses; (c) an "old master".

CHAPTER VI

1. Reconcile the following statements:

(a) The value of an article depends on supply and demand.

(b) The value of an article approximates to its costs of production.

(c) The value of an article is determined by its marginal utility.

2. Since salt is essential to life and silver is not, show how it is that salt is less valuable per ounce than silver.

3. What is a market? What are the conditions of a good market? Does the labour market fulfil these conditions?

4. What is meant by saying that demand and supply are in a state of equilibrium? Describe the process by which a price level is reached in the open market.

5. Distinguish between market price and normal price. Under what conditions are they likely to coincide?

CHAPTER VII

1. What do you understand by monopoly? Explain the effect of a monopoly on the fixing of the price of an article.

2. Compare the positions of a monopolist and a competing producer with regard to (a) the factors influencing the output each will place on the market, and (b) the extent to which each affects market price.

3. In what circumstances do you consider that a monopoly is justifiable? What are the essentials of a monopoly?

4. What do you understand by dumping? Why do manufacturers find such a policy profitable?

5. " The monopolist is no different from the competing producer for they both aim at maximum profits." Why, then, should the monopolist be subject to control?

CHAPTER VIII

1. " Money is as money does." Explain this statement.

2. What factors determine the demand for money and the supply? What is the effect of changes in the velocity of circulation of money?

3. Which is more likely to benefit an industrial nation —a period of rising prices or a period of falling prices?

4. Discuss the functions of money.

5. What are the functions of a modern bank? Estimate the economic importance of banking to industry.

CHAPTER IX

1. What is the connection between rent and cost?

2. What do you understand by economic rent? Is the term applicable to the payment made for the occupation of a dwelling?

3. Examine the plea of the shopkeeper in a main thoroughfare that he is compelled to charge a higher price than shopkeepers in back streets because he pays a higher rent.

4. " Economic rent, both rural and urban, arises from the same cause." Consider this statement.

5. What is the National Income? Who is entitled to a share of it?

CHAPTER X

1. To what extent can a trade union raise the wages of its members?

2. Do you agree that a person's income is not what he gets, but what that income will buy?

3. Why do skilled workers normally receive higher wages than unskilled workers? How do you explain the fact that in times of depression a dustman may receive higher wages than many skilled engineers?

4. What would be the effect on wages of—

(a) a steady decline in the size of working class families;
(b) a cheapening of the necessaries of life?

5. What principles govern the determination of wages? Account for differences in wages in different occupations.

CHAPTER XI

1. What factors determine the rate of interest? What would be the effect of a fall in the rate of interest on the prices of (a) land; (b) port wine; (c) houses?

2. " The greater the supply of capital available, the less productive is the use to which it can be put." Discuss this statement.

3. Why is the return upon investment in ordinary shares normally higher than the return upon investment in fixed interest securities?

4. What factors determine the accumulation of capital?

5. Is there any economic justification for the payment of interest on loans?

CHAPTER XII

1. Profits are calculated upon capital but are not due to capital. For what economic service are profits paid?

2. Why does profit differ in (a) different industries; (b) the same industry?

3. What are profits? Show how they emerge and the nature of the service rendered by the ordinary shareholder so as to entitle him to a share of such profits.

4. Who is the entrepreneur in a public company? What is the service he performs?

5. What is the difference between interest and profits? How would you distinguish between the services performed by the receiver of interest and the receiver of profit?

CHAPTER XIII

1. What is meant by the statement that " exports must pay for imports "? Is it possible for a country to import more than it exports?

2. Why does trade arise between different nations?

3. How is the rate of exchange between two currencies determined in the long run?

4. What do you understand by an " infant industry "? Consider the desirability of protecting such an industry against foreign competition.

5. Do you consider that it is possible for a country to be self-sufficing?

CHAPTER XIV

1. " Every old tax is a good tax; every new tax begins by being a bad tax." Consider this statement.

2. What are " rates "? Do you consider that local taxation conforms with the rule of ability to pay?

3. Which do you consider to be the essential functions of a modern State? What other functions may it assume?

4. What are the principal sources of national revenue? Compare taxation and borrowing from the point of view of their effect on production.

5. What is a tax? Do you consider the British Income Tax conforms with the principles of a good tax? Consider the business man's view that a high income tax is a burden on industry.

BIBLIOGRAPHY

The following list of authorities and of selected works is intended to guide those readers who desire to make a more detailed study of Economic Science or of one of its branches.

GENERAL WORKS

Benham, F.   . *Economics.*
Cairncross, A.   . *Introduction to Economics.*
Croome and King *Livelihood of Man.*
Eastham, J. K. . *An Introduction to Economic Analysis.*
Galbraith, J. K. . *The Affluent Society.*
Hanson, J. L.   . *A Textbook of Economics.*
Hicks, J. R.   . *The Social Framework.*
Nevin, E. J.   . *Textbook of Economic Analysis.*
Speight, H.   . *Economics: the Science of Prices and Incomes.*
Stonier and Hague *Textbook of Economic Theory.*

CLASSICAL TREATISES

Malthus, T.   . *Essay on Population.*
Mill, J. S. .   . *Political Economy.*
Ricardo, D.   . *The Principles of Political Economy and Taxation.*
Smith, Adam   *Wealth of Nations.*

ADVANCED GENERAL WORKS

Boulding, K.   . *Economic Analysis.*
Chamberlin, E. . *Theory of Monopolistic Competition.*
Keynes, J. M. . *General Theory of Employment, Interest and Money.*
Knight, F. H. . *Risk, Uncertainty and Profit.*
Lipsey, R. G. . *Positive Economics.*
Marshall, A.   . *Principles of Economics.*
  Do.   . *Industry and Trade.*
Pigou, A. C.   . *The Economics of Welfare.*
Robbins, L.   . *The Nature and Significance of Economic Science.*

Robinson, Joan .   *Theory of Employment.*
Samuelson, P. A.   *Economics.*
Stigler, G. .   .   *Theory of Price.*
Wicksteed, P.   .   *The Commonsense of Political Economy.*

SPECIALISED WORKS ON VARIOUS BRANCHES

Value and Distribution

Carver, T. N. .   .   *Distribution of Wealth.*
Henderson, H. D. .   *Supply and Demand.*
Hicks, J. R. .   .   *Value and Capital.*

The Theory of Money and Prices

Crowther, G. .   .   *An Outline of Money.*
Day, A.   .   .   *Outline of Monetary Economics.*
Robertson, D. H. .   *Money.*
Stewart, M. .   .   *Keynes and After.*
Tew, B.   .   .   *International Monetary Co-operation.*

Credit, Banking and Foreign Trade

Bagehot, W. .   .   *Lombard Street.*
Harrod, R. F.   .   *International Economics.*
Hawtrey, R. G. .   *Currency and Credit.*
King, W. T. C. .   *History of the London Discount
                      Market.*
Lavington, F.   .   *The English Capital Market.*
Macrae, N. .   .   *The London Capital Market.*
Sayers, R. S. . . *Modern Banking.*
Thorne, W. A.   .   *Banking.*

Industrial Problems

Allen, G. C. .   .   *British Industries and their Organisa-
                        tion.*
Barou, N.   .   .   *British Trade Unions.*
Beveridge, Lord .   *Full Employment in a Free Society.*
Dalton, H. .   .   *The Inequality of Incomes.*
Florence, P. Sargent   *Labour.*
Hawtrey, R. G. .   *Trade and Credit.*

Hayek, F. A. . . *Monetary Theory and Trade Cycle.*
Hobson, J. A. . *Incentives in the New Industrial Order.*
Hoxie, R. F. . . *Scientific Management and Labour.*
Pigou, A. C. . . *Industrial Fluctuations.*
Robertson, D. H. . *The Control of Industry.*
Robinson, E. A. G. *Structure of Competitive Industry.*
Webb, B. and S. . *Industrial Democracy.*
Do. . . . *The Consumers' Co-operative Movement.*

Public Finance and Taxation

Dalton, H. . . *Public Finance.*
Hicks, U. . . *Public Finance.*
Robinson, M. E. . *Public Finance.*
Stone, R. & G. . *National Income and Expenditure.*

Economic History

Ashton, T. S. . *The Industrial Revolution, 1760–1830.*
Briggs and Jordan . *Economic History of England.*
Chambers, J. D. . *The Workshop of the World.*
Clapham, J. H. . *An Economic History of Modern Britain.*
Cole and Postage . *The Common People, 1746–1946.*
Court, W. H. B. . *A Concise Economic History of Britain from 1750 to Recent Times.*
Hobson, J. A. . *Evolution of Modern Capitalism.*
Lipson, E. . . *Growth of English Society.*
Pollard, S. . . *The Development of the British Economy, 1914–1950.*
Rostow, M. W. . *The Stages of Economic Growth.*
Trevelyan, G. M. . *English Social History.*

History of Economic Thought

Gray, A. . . *The Development of Economic Doctrine.*
Ingram, J.K. . *History of Political Economy.*
Price, L. L. . . *History of Political Economy in England.*
Roll, E. . . *History of Economic Thought.*

INDEX